W9-BFC-251

The Top Gear Guide To BRITAIN

RICHARD PORTER

BBC BOOKS

CONT

ENTS

INTRODUCTION

It is a simple fact that Britain is the best country in the world.

Apart from New Zealand. And maybe Canada. But aside from those… oh, wait, Iceland is very nice too. So apart from those countries, and maybe some bits of France and Italy, there is no place better than Britain. Although if you look at those quality of life surveys, you can't discount Norway. So, um… right, let's just agree that if you average it out, Britain is probably the fourth best country in the world. Fact.

For over ten years, *Top Gear* has been travelling all over Britain in the course of making the world's best programme about cars, driving, and three men in smart-casual clothes shouting at each other. So, who better to assemble a guide to Britain itself with all its glories, quirks and multiple words for bread rolls? This book is not only a guide for outsiders; it is an invaluable reference manual for Britons themselves, like a mirror held up to our very souls. Although in this case, a mirror that has been dropped and then run over by a small lorry but don't worry, some bits of it still just about work.

Join us then, as we travel from A–Z cataloguing and making moderately flippant remarks about every aspect of life and living in the best country in the world after New Zealand and probably Canada, although we're having second thoughts about that, and also some bits of France and, oh God, we hadn't even thought about Denmark which is almost certainly better in every way. Look, it's not a competition. Do those other countries have hovering vans and pies and motorway service stations that make everyone look unattractive? Frankly, we don't know. Or care. This book is about Britain. So there.

A

A1, THE

Major British arterial road connecting London to Edinburgh and the longest numbered road in the whole country. True fact! What really sets the A1 apart, however, is that it is not like other major cross-country routes. In some places it is a single carriageway road creeping past people's bedroom windows, at others it becomes an eight-lane superhighway thundering across the countryside. Sometimes it is flat and arrow-straight, sometimes it's as twisty as a mountain pass. Many sections feel like a proper motorway, yet others are weirdly narrow and rudely interrupted by roundabouts. Unlike other major routes with their corporate service stations and generic eateries, the A1 boasts a deranged selection of independent cafes, moderately terrifying lorry stops and the kind of petrol stations behind which they find a murdered body. Plus, for no readily apparent reason, there's a whole section around Bedfordshire which is fringed by sex shops and a disturbingly scruffy-looking lap dancing bar. In short, the A1 is both Britain's greatest and Britain's strangest road.

Welcome to
Scotland

That was all a bit weird,
wasn't it?

AARDVARK PLUMBING

Quaint British tradition in which businesses and services give themselves a name which will put them first in the phone book (see also 1-2-3 Taxis, A1 Joinery, Aaaaaaaaaaargh Dentistry). This policy hinges entirely on the belief that people choose who they want to work on their house, car or face based entirely on whatever they come to first in the alphabet. This probably isn't the case, otherwise we'd all drive Alfa Romeos and go on holiday to Afghanistan. This tradition is sure to die out since no one uses the phone book any more and when they need a plumber they are more likely to search for one on the internet. As a result, small businesses will adapt to this social change by re-branding themselves with search-engine-optimised names such as Lindsey Lohan Completely Naked Funeral Services Ltd.

Shops	➡️
More shops	➡️
Other shops	↩️
Different shops	⬇️
(departures)	➡️
Look! Shops!	↘️

AIRPORTS

British airports are the best in the world. This is because they give you something to do whilst you wait for your plane. In contrast, American airports typically offer one small shop and one awful bar and if you go even further afield your only food option is likely to be something unidentifiable served by a hag when really all you wanted was a Pret A Manger. Unfortunately the British have become rather carried away with being good at airports and most modern terminals look more like shopping centres with planes parked outside. This has its limits.

People enjoy buying books or browsing expensive jewellery before they fly. They probably don't want to buy a three-piece suite or a roll-top desk. Still, better that than experiencing a flight delay at Delaware International and realising you've got another three hours of wandering around the same small cubicle that only sells jelly beans and baseball caps then wetting yourself because you didn't know 'restroom' is their word for the lavatory.

ALLEGRO, AUSTIN

Bulbous, unlovely BL family car from the 1970s and staple fallback of lazy comedy writers (see also, Reliant Robin). There is, however, a more serious point to the Austin Allegro beyond giving one to a sitcom character as a heavy-handed way of making clear that they're a twit. This car replaced the pretty, pleasant and very popular Austin 1100/1300 with something that was none of those things. As such, it is a defining moment in the history of our national car industry and indeed our nation as a whole. It is the very textbook example of seizing defeat from the jaws of victory and making a right old cock of things.

AMERICANS, BRITISH PEOPLE WHO SPEAK LIKE

The United States of America is a tremendously exciting place, what with its stridently coloured clothing, drive-in lavatories and constant fear of shooting. For some British people this excitement is too much to bear and manifests itself not in a desire to emigrate but rather to bring a small slice of the US to Britain by line dancing, driving a specially imported American car or, worst of all, speaking like an actual American. Tell-tale signs of this latter condition include saying things like 'apartment', 'licence plate' and 'Hey, can I get a Bud?' instead of the correct British terms 'flat', 'number plate' and 'Excuse me, do you have any beer that has an actual flavour to it?' Rationally speaking, this is all entirely harmless. Less rationally, these people are idiots and should be forced to go and work in a poisonous gas factory in the middle of Idaho until they bloody well grow up.

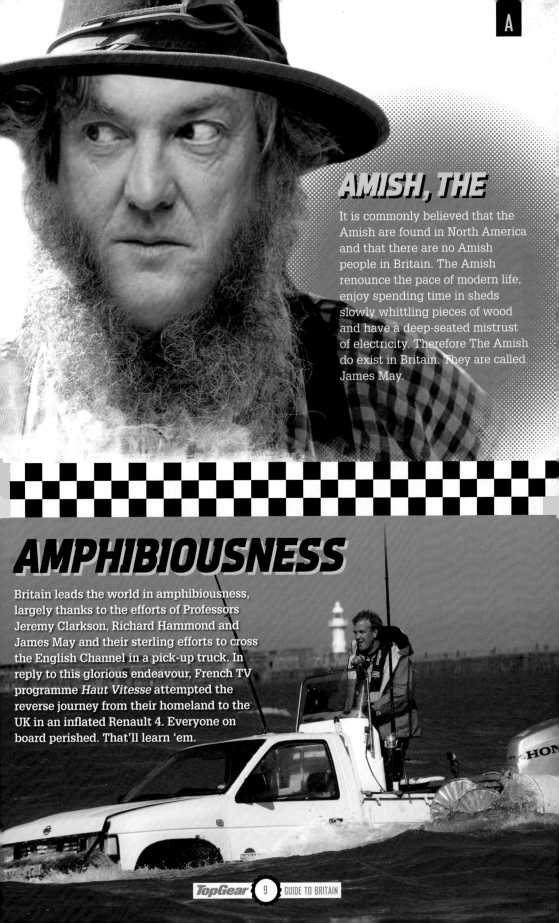

AMISH, THE

It is commonly believed that the Amish are found in North America and that there are no Amish people in Britain. The Amish renounce the pace of modern life, enjoy spending time in sheds slowly whittling pieces of wood and have a deep-seated mistrust of electricity. Therefore The Amish do exist in Britain. They are called James May.

AMPHIBIOUSNESS

Britain leads the world in amphibiousness, largely thanks to the efforts of Professors Jeremy Clarkson, Richard Hammond and James May and their sterling efforts to cross the English Channel in a pick-up truck. In reply to this glorious endeavour, French TV programme *Haut Vitesse* attempted the reverse journey from their homeland to the UK in an inflated Renault 4. Everyone on board perished. That'll learn 'em.

AMUSING TIES

The British are great fans of the 'comedy' tie and over the years they have embraced many light-hearted designs, from the mock piano keyboard to items involving Garfield the cartoon cat. The jocular tie is a great way for an office-bound man to show that he is not a corporate slave and still has a vibrant and unique personality despite the strictures of his employers' dress code. All of which is fine, just as long as you remember that all 'funny' ties are in fact not remotely funny and anyone who wears one should be flayed to death with mooring rope.

APOLOGISING

Britain leads the world when it comes to apologising. In fact, it is estimated that the average British person says the word 'sorry' more than any other, and that includes other commonly used words such as 'the', 'and' and 'ungulates'. Such is the British devotion to saying sorry that they will even use it after someone else has stepped on their foot. This is no mere affectation but a reflection of British manners and, in this case, an acceptance that it was bloody stupid to leave your foot lying around under the edge of the table just waiting to get stepped on. On a grander scale, the British are forever apologising on the world stage too. Every so often the Prime Minister will stand up during a visit to another country and deliver a heartfelt apology for something that the British did in the past. The residents of the foreign land will look bemused at this. They may protest that it does not bring back their slain compatriots, return the disputed lands or suck the pollutants from the river but that's not the point. The British need to apologise. Otherwise it plays on their mind and they can't sleep. So just take the apology and stop making such a fuss.

Ways in which only the British can use the word sorry

'Sorry, you seem to have shot me'

'Sorry, I think your son might be attacking me.'

'Sorry, is it possible for you to reverse your car off me?'

'Sorry, would you mind ceasing your affair with my wife?'

'Sorry, do you know when you'll be finished burgling us?'

APOSTROPHES

The apostrophe is handy piece of punctuation typically used to denote the absence of a letter in contracted words such as 'it's' and 'they're'. In Britain, however, the apostrophe has now become something of moving target, often disappearing from the words in which it has a rightful place, only to show up in places where, technically speaking, it is not required such as 'CD's' and 'bargain's galore'. If you are relaxed about such things this is simply the natural evolution of language and nothing to be worried about. If, however, you are a grammar purist this is a disgusting smear on the very fabric of our society and anyone who perpetuates it is a vile, stupid, thoughtless waste of blood and oxygen who should have their head placed into a stout canvas sack and then bludgeoned repeatedly with stout bats. Take your pick.

ARCHERS, THE

Long-running radio serial which, according to Richard Hammond, is much loved and, according to James May, is the single worst thing in Britain and the utter ruination of the entire country with its fatuous and sentimental depictions of a countryside that never existed, and into which they make patronising and inept gestures towards modernity by randomly mentioning 21st century things even though the entire programme seems to inhabit some sort of mythical, idiotic and profoundly annoying 1950s dreamworld.

```
                    The Archers
                  Episode 47,458
                     Scene 1


Old Geoff
Yaaaarp. Seems to be some reed flies up in yon field thar.


Young Peter
Aye. Be a storm brewin' too. I hope mine crops don't take
a batterin', it be harvest time soon.


Old Geoff
Aye. I feel it in my knee Young Peter, thar definitely be
some weather on the way.


Young Peter
Aye. I hope it don't spoil the barn dance tonight. I be
hopin' far a dance with young Wendy, I do.


Old Geoff
Aye. I knows you got your eye on her for a wife, young
Peter. Don't worry, if rationing can't stop the barn dance
then I be sure that a bit of rain won't stop it neither.
Shall I check the weather forecast on my iPad Mini?
```

ARIEL

Shed-based creator of wonderful, skeletal sports cars. Also the only car maker based in Somerset. As a result, unfounded rumours persist that next year they will launch a 'dual-fuel' model that can run on both petrol and cloudy cider.

ARSE

The Americans say ass, which is a type of low-spec donkey and, thanks to the prevalence of their films and television programmes, the rest of the world seems to follow suit. That leaves Britain to enjoy its arse in peace, which is good, because it's a much more expressive word. For example, describing someone as 'an ass' is to suggest that they've been a bit silly or foolish. To describe them as 'an arse' can be all that and so much more, up to and including a monumental berk, all depending on tone and delivery. And, in a way, that is what defines the richness of British English and of the British themselves. We are defined by our arse.

ASTON MARTIN

Once upon a time Aston Martin made lusty old warhorses built from raw meat and church pews. More recently they've got more high tech and now sell achingly beautiful sports cars precisely constructed with aluminium extrusions and lasers. Either way, a person cannot consider themselves truly British unless they get a tingly mixture of pride and excitement upon seeing an Aston, even if the Aston in question is on the hard shoulder with steam coming out of it.

AUSTRALIANS

Australia is a perfectly nice place. It's a bit hot and it's packed with creatures that want to bite and/or poison you but even so, there's a lot to recommend it, not least Australians themselves who are an affable bunch with a positive outlook and a can-do attitude. Unfortunately, when Australians move to the UK much of this goes out of the window and they spend their entire time moaning about the weather and telling people how much better things are 'back home' (while conspicuously not going back there). In going through the simple act of constantly complaining about something whilst secretly quite liking it, the UK-based Aussie reveals one important fact about themselves; at heart, they are British all along.

B IS O ARS

The trading name of Bristol Cars, at least according to the constantly malfunctioning illuminated sign on their London premises. For years Bristol pedalled slightly unusual luxury cars for slightly unusual people (including celebrity customers like Richard Branson and Liam Gallagher) until they realised there weren't enough slightly unusual people to make that a valid business model, at which point they popped outside with their service revolver to bring the whole beastly affair to an end. Fortunately, although there isn't much call for new Bristols, there is still a steady demand for the purchase and/or restoration of old second-hand Bristols which is why their London premises and that famous sign exist to this day. HOOR H!

Cheshire-based company who, despite their home county, do not sell cars with fake pillars or onyx drinks globes or that only come with bodywork in orange. In fact, their one model, the Mono, is as crisp, light and beautifully detailed as a Swedish dental surgery.

D

Wor

Issue: 2401

First Edi

BARBECUES

The barbecue encapsulates almost everything there is about being British; hospitality, stoicism, bloody-mindedness, and a love of crap, badly-cooked food. If you want to see the classically British facet of grim determination in the face of unfavourable odds look not to the Battle of Agincourt or the Dunkirk evacuation but merely observe a British person attempting to light a barbecue in the rain on a grey Saturday afternoon in June, even though he knows full well that there is a grill and an oven just yards away in his own kitchen, both of which he could use to cook food in a manner that wouldn't give all his friends botulism.

AILY FAIL

Business - Finance - Lifestyle - Travel - Sport - Wea

THE WORLDS BEST SELLING NATIONAL NEWSPAPER

Mo

MURDER!
BEARDS

Britain has a long history of bearded men in the public eye stretching from King Charles I and John Lennon to Peter Sutcliffe and Harold Shipman. In other words, if you have a beard you will probably be killed or sent to prison for murder. Bad news for Noel Edmonds. Or good news, depending on your point of view.

BEER

British beer is one of those unique things about Britain that consistently baffles foreigners. Yet in many ways, proper British beer is like a flat, boozy window into the very soul of Britain itself since it too is strange, lukewarm and damp. People from overseas, used to their light and effervescent lagers, can be forgiven for thinking that British beer is wilfully unappetising, but that is to forget that the British are a people raised on drizzle and lard. In other words, they genuinely like this stuff.

BELL END

A short street in the village of Wollaston, Northamptonshire which is constantly having its sign stolen. No one knows why.

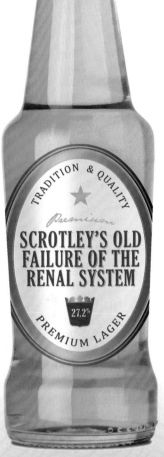

ORIGINAL RECIPE

SUMMER BLINDNESS
6.8%

BREWED WITH PASSION FOR QUALITY

SLOW PAINFUL
DEATH
BY
BEES
12.9%

TRADITION & QUALITY

Premium

SCROTLEY'S OLD FAILURE OF THE RENAL SYSTEM
27.2%

PREMIUM LAGER

BENTLEY

Cheshire's other car-maker and seller of expensive things to the starting eleven of most Premiership football sides. Despite the association with ball-kicking buffoons, modern Bentleys are rather excellent, being beautifully trimmed, stoutly constructed and not at all short of power. As a result, driving one gives you a very real sense of what it would be like to thunder past a caravan whilst sitting inside Chatsworth House.

Wish you were here!

BIRMINGHAM

A large West Midlands conurbation and England's second city. Birmingham is famed for several things including TV's Richard Hammond, men with big sideburns standing around a brazier, and an accent that makes even wedding vows and Oscar acceptance speeches sound like nasal moaning about having to do the washing up. People from Birmingham like to say that the city has more canals than Venice and more parks than Paris. This might be true. No one from the rest of the country can be bothered to check. More importantly, even if the canals ran with wine and the parks were made of solid gold, they would still be in Birmingham.

MATRIS QUOD ABBAS DON'T AMO VOS

BOARDING SCHOOL

Boarding schools stem from a great British tradition of finding your own children slightly annoying and not wanting to see them very much until they are at an age when they want to leave home anyway. Jeremy went to boarding school. From this we can conclude that going to boarding school makes you prone to exaggeration and setting things on fire.

BOLLOCKS

Technically, another word for testicles.
Actually, a hugely versatile term that can
suggest a thing is rubbish, that a person is
talking nonsense, that everything is wrong
or that great courage has been shown.
Bollocks is possibly the most British word
in the entire English language simply
because no one outside of Britain, no matter
how long they have spoken English nor
how well they have mastered it, is capable
of using it with conviction. It just makes
them sound like they're talking… etc etc.

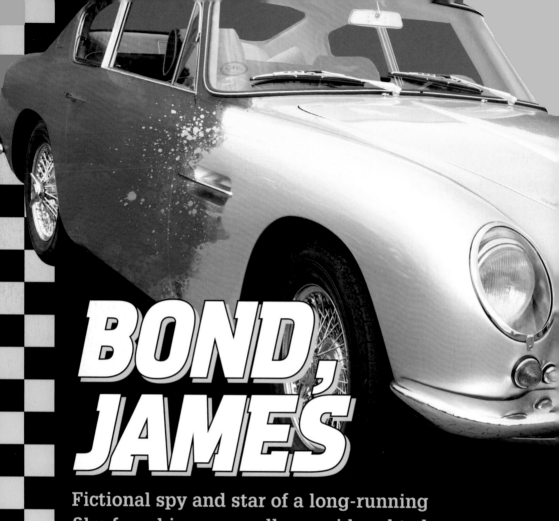

BOND, JAMES

Fictional spy and star of a long-running film franchise, generally considered to be a British hero. In fact, James Bond has completely ruined several aspects of British life. Because of him, all restored Aston Martin DB6s get sprayed silver, all people ordering a vodka martini have to make an idiotic proviso about the way in which it is mixed, and all men putting on a dinner suit start to think they are a suave international baddie-killer rather than, as is usually the case, a fat loss-adjuster from Marlow.

BRANSON, RICHARD

The people's capitalist, Richard Branson has long ignored the traditional British feeling that making lots of money is a bit vulgar, and yet avoided the sneering hatred of the entire nation by the simple expedient of dressing in a casual manner. A valuable tip for others; if you want to do something terribly un-British and still be liked, simply do it in a chunky jumper.

BROGUES

Stout and classically British shoe much favoured by James May. In 1990 this type of footwear inspired a chart-topping song by the popular American singer Madonna, although she slightly changed the title at the last minute.

BROWN SIGNS

A uniquely British way of guiding people towards alarmingly dull ways to waste a Sunday afternoon. Obviously some brown signs direct you to excellent things like tank museums or motor-racing circuits but rather more of them point towards something that turns out to be less interesting than listening to James May describe how a camshaft works.

Owl Crematorium

Cress Museum

World of Rats

The Big Fence

James May Describes How a Camshaft Works

BUBLÉ, MICHAEL

Smooth voiced crooner, seemingly incapable of knotting a neck tie properly. Popular all over the world but especially in Britain where ladies of a certain age can enjoy his slick American razzmatazz safe in the knowledge that he's actually Canadian and therefore won't suddenly loose off a handgun into the ceiling.

C

CAKE

The hefty, tasty, jammy or fruity foundation for much of what Great Britain was, is and will be. A British person could be facing the darkest night of the soul, staring down the barrel of social exclusion, financial ruination and the recent death of their faithful dog. But offer them a slice of cake and suddenly things don't seem so bad, do they? See also; Tea, a nice cup of.

CANAL BOATING

Britain was one of the first countries in the world to build a canal network, initially to permit the transport of goods and latterly to give couples of a certain age the excuse to put on jaunty, nautical-looking hats and putter about for an entire week in a brightly painted boat, at the end of which they will have covered a distance no greater than 12 miles. The British canal network is ample, but it is also extremely narrow which is why canal boats always appear to be 100 feet long and about three feet wide, rather like the Jaguar XJS. British canals are also quite shallow which is why canal boats have flat bottoms, and this in turn explains why if you ever see one on the open water of a river or the sea it looks like it is about to capsize. No other country in the world is as enthusiastic about canal boating as the British nor maintains that enthusiasm with such gritted teeth, even when they realise they have inadvertently moored up after sundown in a highly industrialised area just outside Wolverhampton and are now having stolen bicycles dropped on them by some local youths.

CATERHAM

The daddy of British small sports car-makers with a business model based around the very simple idea of taking an old Lotus design and then gently refining it over the course of 40 years. Of course, driving a Caterham is never going to make you look anything less than a bit nerdy, but if you like driving then this is the best place to get a pure shot of neat, distilled drivingness. Just do it where no one else can see you.

CHESHIRE

A North Western county which has given the nation many things including dairy products, aircraft and a significant contribution to our supplies of road salt. Unfortunately, thanks to the influx of footballers and people who are married to footballers, certain parts of Cheshire are amongst the most ghastly places in the country and home to more marble and onyx than anywhere else, making this county by far the heaviest in Britain. If a foreigner arrived in the UK and went straight to Wilmslow they may erroneously assume that the British are entirely orange.

CHEESE

The British like cheese a great deal and embrace a whole range of cheeses from a light, crumbly Caerphilly to a creamy and complex Red Leicester. However, the real heart and soul of British cheese appreciation lies in stout, pungent lumps of mouthwatering mould like Stilton and Shropshire Blue. As a result, where other nations prize cheeses with qualities such as 'delicate' or 'smooth', the ideal British cheese is best described as 'fighty'.

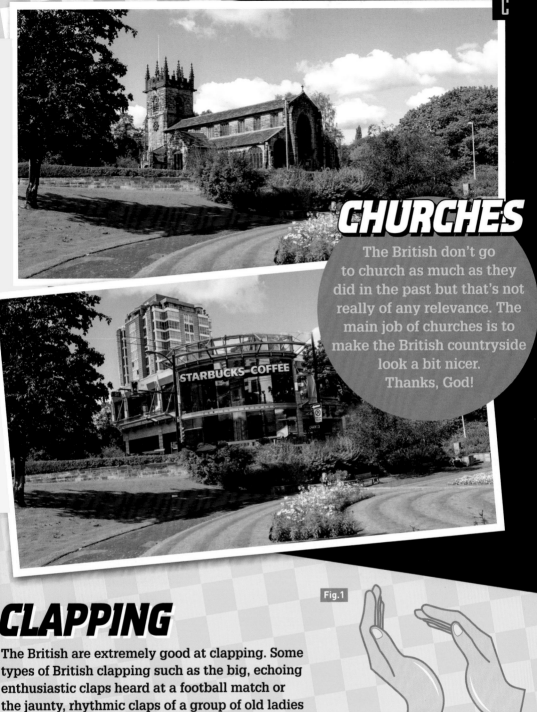

CHURCHES

The British don't go to church as much as they did in the past but that's not really of any relevance. The main job of churches is to make the British countryside look a bit nicer. Thanks, God!

CLAPPING

The British are extremely good at clapping. Some types of British clapping such as the big, echoing enthusiastic claps heard at a football match or the jaunty, rhythmic claps of a group of old ladies listening to the *Horse Of The Year Show* theme music can be heard at other events in other countries. However, there is one type of clapping that is only heard in Great Britain and that's the crisp, light, short-lived clatter of applause heard during a village cricket match. It is utterly unique and there probably should be a word for it. 'Crattle'. That would be a good one. No? Please yourselves.

Fig.1

Fig.2

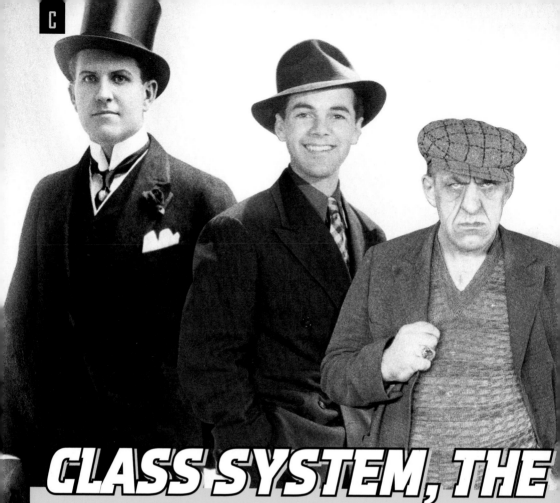

CLASS SYSTEM, THE

Many countries all but eradicated their class system by the simple expedient of rounding up their upper classes and then cutting their heads off. Many others operate a social structure based simply on how much money you have. In Britain, however, things are MUCH more complicated than that. Money has very little to do with it since many British toffs have almost no cash at all, and what little they do possess is immediately swallowed by the vast, drafty wreck of a house they have wearily inherited from nine previous generations of their family. Conversely, someone can make a lot of money, live in a large house, drive a very expensive car and still be refused entry to certain types of club because they have a trace of an accent and the wrong sort of shirt cuffs. As a result of all this complexity, British people are practically born with an in-built class radar which enables them to make swingeing value judgements about others based on their shoes, cutlery use and the word they employ when asking where the lavatory is.

IDENTIFY A BRITISH PERSON'S CLASS

In modern Britain an upper-class person might be identified by their sense of entitlement, their rudeness to others and their rampant substance abuse problems. A working-class person can be identified by their sense of entitlement, their rudeness to others and their rampant substance abuse problems. That leaves middle-class people who can be identified by their obsession with school catchment areas and their determination to conduct all furious rows with their partner in an intense hiss whilst standing in the middle of IKEA.

CLOSING TIME

Despite changes to licensing laws, most British pubs still close at 11pm. This is a throwback to The Great War and was part of an attempt to stop factory workers getting sloshed when they had important things like artillery shells to make the next day. A source of much bemusement and hilarity amongst visiting foreigners, closing time is one reason why the British are so good at drinking heartily yet quickly, often with one eye on their watches. In a pub full of all nationalities, the British man can be identified as the one who hears the landlord call for everyone to leave his premises, says 'Right' in a businesslike manner and then, in one smooth movement, stands up and pulls on his coat whilst simultaneously seeing away the remaining half a pint of beer in his glass. Such casual mannishness takes years of practise.

CONVERTIBLES

The British buy more convertible cars than anyone else in Europe, a fact that seems to baffle some car-industry analysts who smirk with amusement that the people with the lousiest weather seem the most determined to become exposed to it. Actually, this isn't a mystery at all. The average Italian or Spanish person knows that they're going to get sunshine for at least half the year and there's no novelty in that. The average British person has simply no idea what the weather is going to be doing from one day to the next. Lashing rain in July? Yep, that could happen. Manic sleet in September? You wouldn't rule it out. But maybe, just maybe, on one or two days every few months the sun might come out, and by God you want to enjoy those moments to the full, even if it means putting up with a noisier, leakier, less secure car for the year.

COOKING

Traditionally, British cooking is like the very soil upon which Britain is built; heavy, thick and slightly damp. It explains dishes such as spotted dick, treacle sponge and a fondness for drowning savoury things in a very thick gravy. These days Britain has of course embracing a vast range of cuisines from other countries, from Italy to Ethiopia, because Britain has always been open and welcoming to other cultures, especially if their food turns out to be much nicer than ours. Despite this, however, any British person who does not at least once a month crave a hearty slice of roast beef with roast potatoes, Yorkshire pudding and all the trimmings is basically guilty of treason.

CORSA, VAUXHALL

A surprisingly popular small hatchback in Britain, the Vauxhall Corsa is more than simply a car. It is, in fact, a way to identify idiots and those who are completely incapable of driving.

MATCH SUMMARY

DAY 105

CRICKET

A game the British exported to their colonies only to discover a few years later that, annoyingly, their colonies had become quite good at it. The British have shown their resilience in many ways over the years, through war and famine and invasion, but nothing demonstrates the strength of the British character more than being able to sit through an entire Test match without slitting your own wrists.

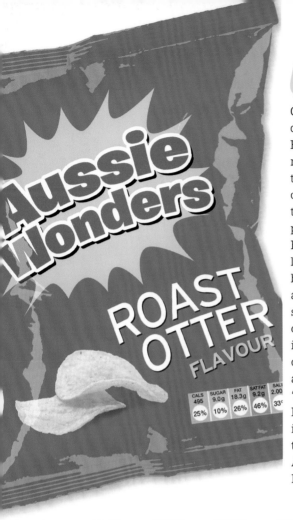

C

CRISPS

Great Britain leads the world in the design and manufacture of crisps. A British person visiting any country in mainland Europe is typically staggered at the poor selection of styles and flavours of crisp, usually running to a maximum of three different sorts, one of which is plain and therefore doesn't count. Former British colonies such as Australia are a little better but they often get the flavour-based colour coding of the packets wrong and spear off in recipe directions that no sane person would want such as roast otter or ants on toast. The United States is even worse, boasting a deranged obsession with bright orange colouring and endless variations on the theme of 'cheese flavor' when any right-thinking British person knows that all you need in that role is Wotsits. No, Britain leads the world in crisps and that's an end of it. After all, which nation invented the beef Hoola Hoop? Exactly.

CALS	SUGAR	FAT	SAT FAT	SALT
495	9.0g	18.3g	9.2g	2.00
25%	10%	26%	46%	33%

Aussie Wonders
ROAST OTTER FLAVOUR

CYCLING

In recent years Britain has been having a good run of things, cycling-wise. Olympic gold medals, hireable bikes in major cities, a win in the Tour de France without resorting to being a mono-bollocked drug cheat. Unfortunately, all of these excellent cycling developments have been completely undermined by one piece of utterly inexplicable and frankly terrifying news: Some time in early 2013, Jeremy Clarkson bought a bicycle. In response, a panicked Vatican began an immediate investigation just to make doubly sure that the Pope is indeed on their team.

D

2002

1998

2009

DAVE

A British television station, so-named because apparently everyone knows someone called Dave. Slavishly devoted to showing repeats of *Top Gear* which is enjoyable for many but a nightmare for Jeremy Clarkson, Richard Hammond or James May, who see Dave not as a TV channel but as one, massive, horrible flashback.

2013

DIRECTIONS

In Japan, people go out of their way to help others who are lost. The same is true in India but with even more friendliness, to the point where an innocent request for directions will find you five hours later at the wedding of a complete stranger. The British, being more withdrawn, cannot match these lofty levels of good grace and selflessness, but natural British reserve can't mask the natural British politeness which manifests itself when someone doesn't know directions to the place they have been asked about. Rather than say, 'I'm sorry, I've no idea where that is,' the average British person must go through an enormous pantomime of face pulling, chin scratching and elaborate shrugging in order to show that they are doing their level best to think about where this elusive street might be before finally, with a flamboyant show of cheeky puffing and eye rolling, they must admit that they have not been able to dredge it from the recesses of their mind. For these complex performances alone, everyone in Britain should really have at least one Oscar.

DEFINITELY

OR IS IT

LEFT

RIGHT?

DISSEMBLING

Not to be confused with 'disassembling' which is what Jeremy Clarkson does to his 'completely broken' iPhone with a hammer before remembering that he's forgotten to switch it on. Dissembling is defined as concealing your true feelings and is essentially the entire basis for 78 percent of all conversations that happen in Britain.

DIY

The British like nothing more than to spend their weekends driving down to their nearest branch of B&Q or Homebase, buying a load of parts and tools that they don't really understand, and then going home in order to use them to make some part of their own house slightly worse. This national obsession with 'doing it yourself' is particularly enjoyed by professional plumbers, electricians, and builders, and anyone else who earns their living coming into your house to re-do the job properly.

DOCTORS

From discovering penicillin to mapping the human genome, Britain has made some major contributions to health care which is all the more remarkable when you consider that, upon visiting their GP and being asked how they are, the average British person could have a gaping hole in their head or an entire arm hanging off and still reply, 'Fine, thanks'.

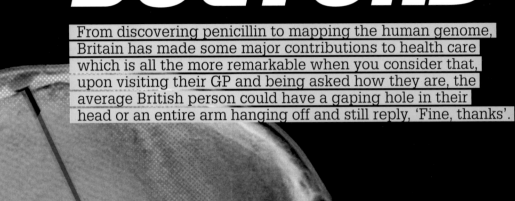

Never felt better, Doc

DOGS

The British are extremely fond of dogs. In fact, it is estimated that up to 93 percent of all rhetorical questions in Britain are asked by people talking to dogs and includes classics such as 'Who's a good boy?' 'Are you hungry?' and 'Do you want the ball? Do you? Do you? Do you? Yes you do. Yes. You. Doooo.' As the map on this page shows, a remarkable number of dog breeds are named after places in Britain, and from this we can conclude that the dog was actually invented in Britain. Probably.

YORKSHIRE TWATHOUND

IPSWICH DINGO

LINCOLNSHIRE SPUDHOUND

LONDON GENTLEMAN

BERKSHIRE BELIEBER

GEORDIE SHORE

DRIVING

The British are the best in the world at driving. This is a fact. In truth, the British have little competition for their excellence when you consider their rivals. The Americans are forever inattentively drinking oversized coffees and using their mobile phones at the same time and even when they don't, they can't drive around corners. The Germans boast about their derestricted autobahns but gloss over the fact that they're constantly crashing on them. The Australians are ruthlessly limited to the equivalent of 49mph and half asleep at the wheel as a result. The French, the Italians and the Spanish are too erratic. The Belgians are utterly hopeless, as you'd expect from a nation that didn't make the driving test mandatory until 1977. The Scandinavians think they're brilliant and yet conveniently forget that every other shop in Sweden and Norway has a crashed van poking out of the front. And as for the rest of the world, they're still getting the hang of it. Ergo, no one on earth is as good at driving as the British.

DUNGENESS

A Kentish coastal town with an enormous beach and therefore a natural tourist attraction. Except that there's a massive nuclear power station there too. Now, in other countries that would drive away all visitors. But not in Britain. In Britain, it is STILL a natural tourist attraction. Just one with a huge source of radiation slap bang in the middle of it, mere yards away from people bloody-mindedly trying to enjoy a Spam sandwich.

E EDINBURGH FESTIVAL

Annual arts event comprising chiefly of famous comedians honing the material they'll use for their million-selling Christmas DVDs and gangs of students putting on avant-garde productions called things like *The Loneliness Of The Company Of Friends* which consist of two men in boiler suits staring at a sausage roll whilst repeatedly shouting the word 'plinth' for two-and-a-half hours.

THE FUNNY FARM

Presents

A BLUE TOMATO WORKSHOP PRODUCTION

THE LONELINESS OF THE COMPANY OF FRIENDS

It's FREE!

"MAKES YOU REFLECT ON ALL THE OTHER THINGS YOU COULD BE DOING"
THE GUARDIAN

WWW.PLINTHPLINTPLINTH.COM

'VERY LIKELY THAT YOU DO NOT AGREE WITH THIS STATEMENT'

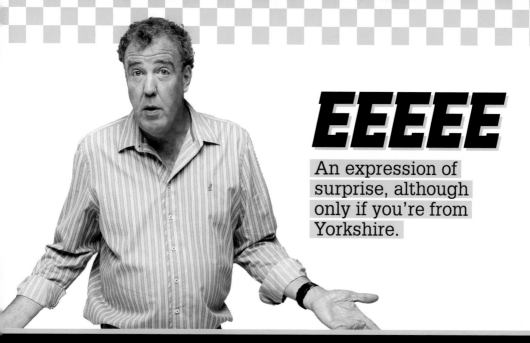

EEEEE

An expression of surprise, although only if you're from Yorkshire.

EMBARRASSMENT

The single biggest driving force in the lives of British people. Embarrassment is what stops the British from talking about money or interrupting conversations or turning around and going back after saying a big goodbye and then realising they have left their jacket behind. If you travel around the world you will encounter British people in almost any country you visit. How have they ended up here, you may wonder? Was it love or employment or a fondness for the scenery that drove them here? In most cases, the answer is no. It's simply that back in Britain they once bumped into someone they had met before and then got their name wrong, causing embarrassment of such magnitude that they were forced to flee the country immediately.

APPLICATION

ENTRY VISA

1. NAME .... Mark Smith ....

2. DATE OF BIRTH .... 24/08/62 ....

3. PLACE OF BIRTH .... UK ....

4. PROFESSION .... Quantity surveyor ....

5. REASON FOR LEAVING COUNTRY .... Faux-pas ....

EMPIRE, THE

Many years ago, the British used to cruise around the world until they found a country that they liked the look of and which had stuff they might want. They would then move in and make it a bit more like home, apart from the weather which they could do nothing about and which was almost always too bally hot. This practise of annexing bits of the world went on for some time until they had laid claim to so many countries it was said that the sun never set on the British empire. Of course, eventually Britain had to give back most of the empire which made a great many British people sad and inclined to keep talking about it in an attempt to prove that Britain was still powerful and important and not crap. However, these people often forget that today, whilst the sun may set on Britain, somewhere in the world there is always an episode of *Top Gear* on the TV. So in a way, Britain won and all foreign countries lost.

ESSEX

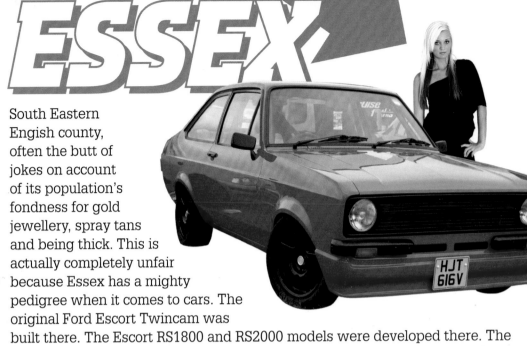

South Eastern Engish county, often the butt of jokes on account of its population's fondness for gold jewellery, spray tans and being thick. This is actually completely unfair because Essex has a mighty pedigree when it comes to cars. The original Ford Escort Twincam was built there. The Escort RS1800 and RS2000 models were developed there. The engine in the legendary Capri 3.0 was actually called the 'Essex' V6. In other words, without Essex we would have been denied some of the greatest fast Fords of all time and therefore the lineage that allows brilliant cars like the Fiesta ST of today. So be thankful for Essex. Even if you think half the people in it are orange idiots.

ESTATE AGENTS

In the United States people who sell houses for a living, 'realtors' as they call them, are perfectly normal members of society. They are respected, invited to parties, waved at cheerfully by postmen. In Britain, however, choosing to sell houses for living is to accept that you will be forever despised by the rest of society. What is it about these hair-gelled, aftershave-sodden, shiny-suited, lying, grasping, obnoxious and incompetent morons that makes them so disliked? Perhaps we will never know.

SONG TITLE	POINTS
BOOM BANGA POP BING POO!	65
MY LOVE SMELLS POWERFUL	63
MAGNIFICENT LADY	57
MAXIMUM SEXY TIME TONIGHT	42
ESPLIMO COOPILSZ	36
WILL THIS DO?	0

EUROVISION

A sort of high camp singing festival which feels like it should have fizzled out in the 1970s. In recent years Britain hasn't taken Eurovision very seriously in the mistaken belief that it's all a joke. In fact, every other European country takes it very seriously indeed, not least because it boasts the highest production values their citizens will see on television all year. As a result of being flippant, Britain usually comes last or nearly last and will continue to do so until it stops mucking about. Or just leaves the rest of Europe to it and puts on a repeat of *Waking The Dead* during Eurovision night.

EXCITEMENT

The British do not, as a general rule, do excitement. Extreme expressions of emotion are something best left to the Spanish or the Americans or some other loudly-spoken people like that. In Britain, joy must be kept well contained and not allowed to disturb the neighbours. Hence, it is quite normal for a British person to calmly describe the single greatest thing they have ever seen in their life as 'quite good'.

F

FARMERS' MARKETS

A relatively new invention in Britain, the farmers' market allows British people to buy the same old things but at twice the price and covered in soil.

LOCAL CABBAGE £150 each

FRESH LEEKS 1.76 KILO | £40 LB

LOCAL SPROUTS .76 KILO | £58.26 LB

SWEE POTA 2.64 Kilo

NEW CROP CARROT 1.10 KILO | £50 LB

FESTIVAL

No one likes a festival more than the British. Garden festivals, poetry festivals, Shakespeare festivals, every summer you can't move in British parks without finding a series of marquees and the smell of ropey outdoor-cooked food as British people attempt to enjoy a faltering rendition of *A Midsummer Night's Dream* or an intense bout of Pam Ayres even though it is pouring with rain. The most enduring of all British festivals is the music festival. Originally, these were really big affairs like Glastonbury, Reading or Donington Monsters Of Rock. Now there seem to be music festivals on every spare bit of open land in the entire country. Indeed, it is estimated that the explosion of music festivals combined with the trend for old bands to reform means that by 2032 there will be more music festivals in Britain than there are people, greatly heightening your chances of coming downstairs one Saturday morning to find Duran Duran playing in your kitchen.

FLOWERS

Flowers are a very British thing. Britain is full of flowers and the British like them so much that they hold flower shows every year. Maybe other countries do that too but their shows probably aren't as nice. After all, there's nothing that flowers like more than being rained on. Historically, the British have shown their love of flowers by writing poetry about them, such as 'Daffodils' by William Wordsworth and 'Ah! Sunflower' by William Blake. In more modern times, they demonstrate their appreciation for flowers by buying them from petrol stations after a blazing row with their wives.

FIGHTING

The British like nothing more than a good fight in a tradition that stretches from the Marquis of Queensberry, who endorsed the rules of modern boxing, right up to Big Dave who sells dodgy DVDs in the back corner of the pub and, according to the landlord, once punched someone so hard their head ended up facing the wrong way. The British love of a good scrap most likely comes from living on an island and regularly having to stop people coming onto it by punching them in the face. In fact, there is only one thing the British like more than punching outsiders and that is punching each other. See your local town centre at around 11:45pm on a Saturday night for details.
See also: war

FISH & CHIPS

The British love fish, from the tiny goldfish that serve as family pets to the majestic carp that inhabit ponds and lakes across the land. However, the ultimate expression of the British love for fish is the way in which they like to catch them, kill them and then wrap them in a thick layer of batter or, as it's sometimes known, a Scottish duvet. This fish is then eaten alongside a hearty portion of extremely heavy, greasy chips using a tiny, splintering wooden fork out of several sheets of paper that the food is slowly turning translucent whilst sheltering from the drizzle in a bus shelter after a night drinking pints of dark brown beer in a dank pub. The British are always baffled when people from other countries don't think this sounds appealing.

FISHING

Fishing is an extremely popular pastime amongst British men who would rather sit on the side of a canal in the rain than be at home. The obvious conclusion from this is that a lot of British men don't like their wives or families.

FORD

Like Heinz baked beans and Kellogg's cornflakes, Ford is mistakenly thought of as British even though it's really American. That said, few companies have as much of a connection to Britain as this one. They might have stopped making cars here, but Ford still designs and develops them in Essex and one in every three cars it sells worldwide has an engine made either in Dagenham or South Wales which is actually pretty remarkable. And every British person has a favourite Ford, usually one of the ace, massively spoilered Cosworth models that really couldn't have been conceived anywhere but Essex.

OPU 742K

PREENING OVERPAID IDIOTS

v

OVER-STYLED HISTRIONIC MORONS

PRICE **£600.28**

KICK OFF **3PM**

Please allow at least 45 minutes before kick off to get tanked up

This ticket entitles the holder to a massive brawl and then a pie on the way home

No refunds, exchanges or cancellation allowed

ADMIT ONE

6250096 5070658 96488

FOOTBALL

Football is a passion across much of Great Britain and it's easy to see why; who wouldn't want to spend an hour and a half watching a cluster of idiots running around, pretending to fall over and then going home to their ghastly orange girlfriends leaving the score at precisely zero apiece. There is in fact much more to football than this and the actual game, genuinely thrilling though it can be when the idiots put their tiny minds to it, can be secondary to everything that football comes with. Going to a football match isn't just about the sport, it's about many other things that the British hold dear: Pubs, beer, fighting and, afterwards, having a pie.

FOREIGNERS

Foreigners are very important to the British and not just to give the *Daily Express* something to moan about on a regular basis. In fact, the British like to pay close attention to what people from other countries are up to. In times past this was to see if the foreigners had any nice stuff which they could pop over and steal. In more recent times the British like to keep on eye on other nationalities so that they can then deride them. In doing so, the British may comfort themselves that, though they won and then lost an empire, at least they don't eat pets and drive on the wrong side of the road.

The Daily Bigot

50p (We'll have none of your silly Euros here thank you very much)

IMMIGRANTS STEALING BRITISH OXYGEN

New study reveals thousands of filthy Europeans are breathing same air as Britain

FORMULA 1

Without Britain there would be no Formula 1. Eight of the current 11 teams are British-based and those who aren't still staff their factories with Brits, which is why Ferrari's Felipe Massa gets his mid-race radio messages through a bloke from Middlesbrough. The British really should be very proud that they lead the world in letting 22 men drive round and round in quick procession looking after their tyres and then going in front of the media looking like a walking billboard to thank their team and sponsors in a flat monotone.

FOXES

In the rest of the world, a fox is an omnivorous animal from the same family as the wolf and the domestic dog. In Britain, however, the fox is rather more complicated than that. Not literally, of course. It's still just a four-legged ginger thing that goes through your bins. Politically, however, the fox is extremely controversial and causes great debate between those who think they should be hunted by packs of dogs and horseback riders as a recreational activity, and those who think such a practise is barbaric. This debate isn't just about the technicalities and moralities of such a thing. It's actually about class and therefore one of the most quintessentially British things in the entire world.

FRUIT & VEG

In most of the world fruit and vegetables are sold in the same way as any other food. In Britain, however, fruit and veg can be obtained either by going to the supermarket as normal or by seeking out a small cluster of stalls and finding the one which sells produce that looks surprisingly fresh considering it has been sitting outside for seven hours and about ten feet from the A1. Under strict but obscure British law, a person is only allowed to become a fruit and veg seller if they are able to shout at a volume slightly louder than a pneumatic drill and can demonstrate the ability to seal a brown paper bag by holding it between both outstretched hands and twirling it round and round.

FUSS, NOT MAKING A

One of the single worst things a British person can do is make a fuss. As far as the British are concerned, fuss-making is what the Italians and the Spanish and other hot-blooded nations do, what with their arm waving and forehead slapping and shouting of things like 'ay ay ayyyy' in the middle of a busy shop. If a British person really does have to draw attention to themselves, and really it's hard to imagine a circumstance in which this would happen, they must preface their attention seeking with a phrase such as, 'Excuse me, I hate to be a nuisance but…' in order to soften the disruption as much as possible. e.g. 'Excuse me, I'm so terribly sorry to disturb you but I'm afraid one of my legs has fallen off.'

G GARDEN CENTRES

The British love going to the garden centre and not necessarily to buy plants, since the average garden centre is officially the most random and confusingly stocked place in Britain. It makes sense to find plants, bags of soil and bird baths on sale in these places. A small café isn't completely silly either. But greetings cards? Clothes? DVDs? There are other shops for such things and ones that do a rather better job of stocking, displaying and selling them than a business whose main trade ought to be begonias and hosepipes.

CHIGFORTH GARDEN CENTRE
Come inside and browse our ample stock!

TODAY WE HAVE SPECIAL OFFERS ON:

Roses!
Bird feeders!
Rabbits!
Scissors!
Hats!
Christmas decorations!
Spoons!
Dinner suits!
Skis!
Church bells!
Bluray players!
Supertankers!
Human organ transplant surgery!
Geese!

GIGS

The British love music and quite rightly too since they are very good at it, especially in the fields of pop and rock. An appreciation of the recorded art naturally leads on to a desire to see the same music being performed live, hence the British fondness for what is usually referred to as 'a gig'. Except by your dad who might attempt to say this word yet, over the course of a single syllable, somehow makes it sound completely wrong. A gig can be a truly excellent experience but it can also be another way in which the British prove their stoicism as, in order to see the live music, they must make their way to a strange part of town and a dank venue with sticky floors and a strange smell of stale sweat which serves beer only in squishy plastic glasses and in which you must watch a mediocre support band and then wait for two hours longer than expected because the actual band are too idle to come on stage at anything close to their allotted time, thereby allowing you to miss your train home which in turn permits you to be mugged whilst looking for a bus stop or cab office. And yet, when asked the next day how the gig was, the average British person will reply that it was 'Great!' and that the band 'Really took the roof off the place'. This is not literally true, though God knows if it was it might make the place smell a bit better.

G

GIN

An alcoholic beverage made from juniper berries which is very popular in Britain for three reasons. Firstly, it gets you quite squiffy. Secondly, it sends you quite mad. Thirdly, what else would you do with juniper berries?

FUN QUIZ! CAN **YOU** IDENTIFY THE JUNIPER BERRY?

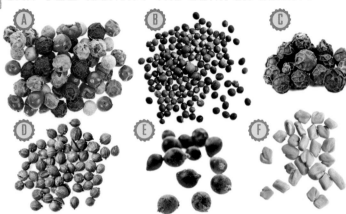

A B C
D E F

GINETTA

Under-rated small sports car maker and unique in that they're based in Yorkshire. As a result, their cars do go on a bit. But on the plus side, they run very happily on tea.

Y J08 NAU

GINGER HAIR

The British have a bit of a problem with red-haired people, often mocking them in a way that seems baffling to people in other nations where hair colour is not considered a rich seam to be mined for personal abuse. It's possible that this curious British attitude derives from an ancient English prejudice against the Scots, Irish and others of Celtic descent since they were more likely to have red hair. Or it might just be that no one likes gingers.

GOLF, THE PASTIME OF

It is often said that golf is 'a good walk, spoiled' but in fact this is not true. Golf is actually a nice piece of countryside spoiled by the inclusion of several sandpits, some eerily smooth bits and a smattering of braying idiots dressed up like Rupert the Bear constantly smacking extremely small but hard balls towards you then retiring to a grotesque mock Tudor bar to swap mildly racist jokes and drink gin & tonics before getting back into their Lexuses to go back to their horrible families in their horrible houses where they can sit back in their horrible conservatories and reflect on just what horrible human beings they are.

GOLF,
THE VOLKSWAGEN

Not a British car but one that has been taken to heart by the British because it neatly sidesteps many of their deep-seated social prejudices and is as close as you can get to a classless car. You wouldn't fear being turned away from a garden party at Sandringham for turning up in a Golf yet nor would you worry for your life if you drove one through the dodgiest parts of Britain's dodgiest towns. As such, the British like the Golf very much because it's one of the few consumer durables that people can't really judge you on. Also, it's a perfectly good functional car and basically what you tell your friends to buy if they ever ask. Need a family car? Get a Golf. Need a second car? Get a Golf. Need a sporty car? Get a Golf GTI. Need a tough 4x4 to safely negotiate the steep, unpaved, three-mile driveway leading to your rural farmhouse, even in the middle of winter? Move to somewhere more civilised and then get a Golf.

GRAVY

The very lifeblood of Britain. Other nations may have their sauce and their jus but only Britain truly understands the wonder of dousing food in a thick, gloopy liquid the colour of a landslide. In fact, why stop at food. If Bisto launched a range of shower gels, shampoos and aftershaves they'd have a runaway success on their hands. Frankly all they'd have to do is mix up some of their existing product and put it in a shower-safe container. Splash a bit of that on and you'd be fighting off Northerners with a stick.

H

HARRUMPH.

HARRUMPHING

Classically British expression of dissatisfaction, best deployed by fat barristers and retired army colonels upon reading something mildly shocking in the *Daily Telegraph*. A really good harrumph should be capable of making a stout volume about submarine warfare fall off a shelf at twenty paces.

HATS

The British suffer a great deal of hat stereotyping from those overseas who imagine that all Englishmen go to work in a bowler hat, all Scotsmen spend their lives in a Tam o'Shanter and that everyone in Wales wears one of these weird hats that looks like a black traffic cone. Plainly, this is not true. In general, the British lost their enthusiasm for all hats back in the 1960s. The main reason for this was the arrival of the baseball cap, which basically makes all British people look idiotic.

HOLIDAY COTTAGES

The British like nothing more than going to stay in someone else's small, slightly chintzy house in another part of the country. Under British law, all rented holiday cottages have to contain a guestbook in which visitors can leave gushing platitudes about the property, the views, the local amenities and the curtains. If you want to unsettle future renters, simply find a guestbook entry that says 'We didn't want to leave!' and write underneath, 'In fact, we haven't. SLEEP WELL'.

The Jackson family, St Albans	A wonderful cottage! We just loved the views, the long walks and the relatively small amounts of gun fire!
Peter & Sue Rees, Cardiff	What a marvellous place! We were charmed by everything about it, especially delightful old Mr Forbisham next door who we have kidnapped and taken home with us!
Alison & David Halfpenny, Ipswich	What a place! Great countryside, great atmosphere! Sorry about what we did to most of the towels!

HOROLOGISTS' SHOPS

Any British town over a certain size will contain a small shop which sells old clocks and watches even though the appetite for such things amongst the majority of the British population is patently quite small. What is the business model here? They must get no more than one paying customer a month and, since the proprietor is clearly 107 years old, it's unlikely that he has a thriving internet shop that keeps things turning over nicely. No, the only explanation for the prevalence of these seemingly pointless shops is that they are some sort of sophisticated, government-sponsored Home Guard and that in the event of nuclear attack or alien invasion, these mild-mannered clock shop owners will lay down their half-moon reading glasses, activate their top-secret, purely mechanical devices disguised as clocks (and thereby impervious to electronic interference), and they will come to save us all. Unless it's Wednesday afternoon. They're closed on Wednesday afternoons.

HORSES

The British like horses very much indeed and for many years have regarded the French penchant for eating them as barbaric and wrong. That is until 2013, when the British discovered that, thanks to some dubious practises in the production of packaged meat products, they had been accidentally scoffing horse for some time. And was this such a bad thing? After all, horses may be noble, beautiful and capable of great feats of speed and endurance but they're also ruddy idiots who get scared by puddles and, let's be honest, until we found out what was in them, we all thought those burgers were actually pretty tasty.

HOT AIR BALLOONS

Not strictly a British invention but on a nice summer's evening in the British countryside, the sight of a hot air balloon drifting gently over the green patchwork quilt of fields makes everything just that little bit nicer. Nicer, that is, for the distant observer rather than for one of the people dangling beneath an enormous exclamation mark in a creaky piece of wicker several hundred feet above the ground with very little steering and a very real chance of clattering into some power lines or simply drifting out over the North Sea, never to return. You can tell the difference between the people on the ground and the people in the basket because the people on the ground are the ones who aren't screaming, 'THIS ISN'T AS RELAXING AS I THOUGHT IT WOULD BE'.

HOVERCRAFT, THE

An air-cushion-based mode of transport that has never really fulfilled its promise because, although it's ingeniously simple, it's also basically a bit daft, strange and pointless. Ergo, the quintessential British invention.

HOVERVAN

A world-beating solution to the problem of flooding in many parts of Britain. A work of genius and striking effectiveness as long as you can ignore the noise, the spray, the danger, the uncontrollability, the fragility, the fuel consumption, the expensive and the ability to damage vast swathes of Warwickshire. Otherwise, brilliant.

1

IANS

It is easy to assume that the success of Britain as a nation is founded on people called things like Henry and Richard and Sir Walter. In fact, Britain would be nothing without chaps like wizardy actor Ian McKellen, short-legged *Lovejoy*-ist Ian McShane, Bondian author Ian Fleming, Jaguar chief designer Ian Callum and ace musicians like monkey-faced Stone Roses frontman Ian Brown, chief Blockhead Ian Dury and flute-toting Jethro Tullist Ian Anderson. That is, in truth, what makes Britain great: Ians.

ICE CREAM VANS

The British summer wouldn't be complete without jangly, slightly distorted renditions of classical music standards and the brightly coloured, slightly diesel-y smelling vans from which they emerge. But hold on a Flaking moment. There's a problem here. Once upon a time there were 25,000 ice creams vans plying their trade in Great Britain. Now, apparently, there are just 500 that actually drive around the place with their tinny chimes and synthetic red-fruit-a-like sauce. Plainly, this is a disaster and something must be done. In fact, something is being done because during 2013 one of the Sunday newspapers started a campaign to right this wrong and get ice cream vans back on our roads for the good of the nation. Strangely, however, they roped in the two blokes from Status Quo as the frontmen for their mission – which means we may see more ice cream vans on our roads but presumably their chimes will be replaced with bogstandard three-chord rock music.

IDIOTS

Britain leads the world when it comes to idiots. The proof of this is in the gurning, mouth-breathing, camera-phone-picture-taking morons who stand behind the presenters and pundits at any televised sporting event or news channel outside broadcast in the UK. For comparison, watch an equivalent live transmission from another country and note that the reporter remains utterly untroubled by cross eyed buffoons shouting 'Oi!' and inbred berks repeatedly mouthing 'Hello mum'. It is therefore a fact: Other countries simply cannot match Britain's high standard of grunting idiot.

INTERNET, THE

The Internet was invented in Britain by a small group of scientists who wanted a quick and easy way to share amusing video clips of cats falling into bins and paparazzi photographs of Hollywood actresses showing an accidental amount of sideboob. Unfortunately, it has since been hijacked by the rest of the world for idiotic things like doing business and keeping in touch with loved ones.

Dear Sir,
I am a prince in Rhodesia and I have recently come into the significant sum of 20 shillings. For completely legitimate reasons, I wish to send you a postal order for this amount. Kindly furnish me with your address so that I may do this
Yours,
Prince David Jackson

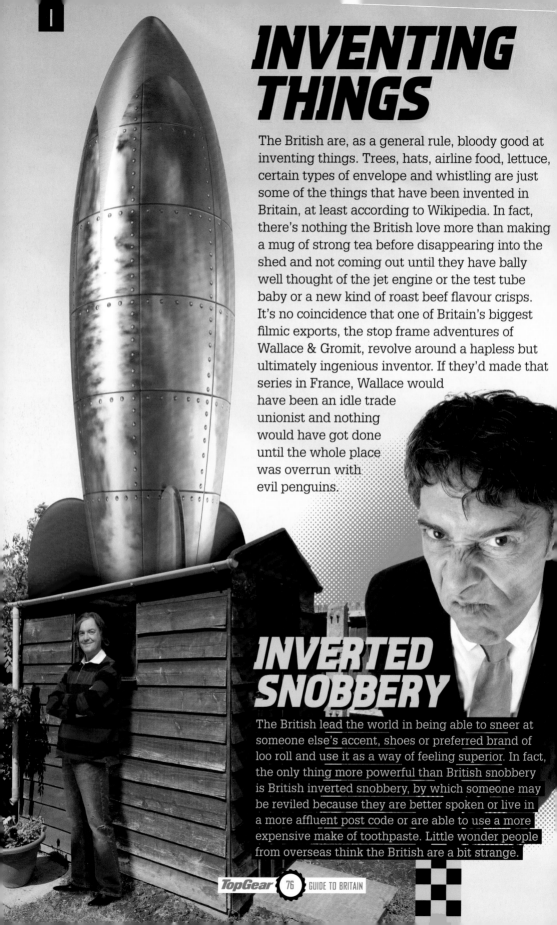

INVENTING THINGS

The British are, as a general rule, bloody good at inventing things. Trees, hats, airline food, lettuce, certain types of envelope and whistling are just some of the things that have been invented in Britain, at least according to Wikipedia. In fact, there's nothing the British love more than making a mug of strong tea before disappearing into the shed and not coming out until they have bally well thought of the jet engine or the test tube baby or a new kind of roast beef flavour crisps. It's no coincidence that one of Britain's biggest filmic exports, the stop frame adventures of Wallace & Gromit, revolve around a hapless but ultimately ingenious inventor. If they'd made that series in France, Wallace would have been an idle trade unionist and nothing would have got done until the whole place was overrun with evil penguins.

INVERTED SNOBBERY

The British lead the world in being able to sneer at someone else's accent, shoes or preferred brand of loo roll and use it as a way of feeling superior. In fact, the only thing more powerful than British snobbery is British inverted snobbery, by which someone may be reviled because they are better spoken or live in a more affluent post code or are able to use a more expensive make of toothpaste. Little wonder people from overseas think the British are a bit strange.

IRISH PUBS

Britain is full of Irish pubs. In this respect it's no different to any other country except that because Britain is very close to Ireland the Irish pubs on its soil fall into two precise categories, being either pubs run by an actual Irish person (usually an affable, barrel-chested bloke called Sean who oscillates between perma-sozzled bonhomie and pitbullish fury towards those who displease him) and pubs run by large corporations who have ordered a job lot of Guinness posters, illuminated shamrocks and double CDs of fiddle music in the vain hope of seeming 'authentic', even though the end result is about as convincingly Irish as Arnold Schwarzenegger shouting 'Top o' ze mornin' to ye'.

Ye Olde Generic O'Patronising

BRITISH THEME PUBS

The Irish have really cornered the market in exporting pub culture to other parts of the world, which seems strange when Britain is a great pub-based nation too. Unfortunately Scottish pubs are rare because landlords make a lot of money out of food and introducing an authentically Scottish menu would immediately have the place closed down by the health inspector. Welsh pubs are unpopular because no one wants to have their drink inadvertently spat in. And there are few English pubs around the world because no one is much interested in brown booze, florid carpets and a jukebox that seems to have 'Going Underground' stuck on a loop.

J JAAAAA

The quintessential mid-level British luxury car. In olden times Jaguars were quite futuristic, then they became tediously obsessed with the past and were wilfully old fashioned, now they've become bang up to date again. In many ways then, Jaguar is just like Britain itself. The main thing about a Jaguar, however, is that whether it's one of the retro ones trimmed in wood and leather and moss, or one of the new, crisply modern aluminium ones, it should be fast and beautiful and give a strong sense that the person driving it has got some stolen artworks in the boot.

JAM

STAWBRY JAM

Sweet, fruity preserve, the small scale manufacture and sale of which makes up over 64 percent of all charitable fundraising in Britain. Probably. As a result, everyone in Britain has at least one jar of crudely labelled jam in the back of the fridge and has spent six years studiously avoiding it because it looks a bit runny and the stuff you get from the supermarket is almost certainly nicer and won't have a finger nail in it.

JAMMY DODGERS

A popular layered biscuit unique to Britain. The contrast between the dry, crumbly biscuit layers and the soft, gooey jam inside brings British people of all ages a feeling of great joy. The enjoyment of two bone-dry biscuits with a gummy red substance between them is yet another reason why people from other countries think British people of all ages are odd.

BUSES

Sorry, this entry has turned up later than you might have hoped.

JEHOVAH'S WITNESSES

A faith system not popular in Britain because it is based around the mistaken belief that people are just waiting to have their dinner interrupted so that they can stand on their own front step letting all the heat out while they make the not inconsiderable decision to adopt a new religion.

JELLY

Brightly coloured gelatin-based wobbly pudding and famed complement to a splodge of ice cream in a British children's party staple. The moment at which it is no longer considered socially unacceptable to scoff down a massive bowl of jelly and ice cream whilst getting much of it across your face is unclear but probably around ten years old. The moment at which you stop actually longing to scoff down a massive bowl of jelly and ice cream whilst getting much of it across your face is never.

JUKEBOXES

Hugely divisive music-playing machines bolted to the walls of many British pubs. Any establishment with a jukebox is basically giving due notice that it is willing to subject its customers to an enormous rollercoaster of emotions as they are forced to endure other people's musical tastes. These will almost certainly include a couple of pale students who will put on Joy Division, Nirvana and at least two other songs by people who have later killed themselves, a bunch of giggling and explicitly squiffy girls who will choose five songs from a compilation CD called *Mmm, That's Some Good Cheese* and finish up with 'Rule The World' by Take That which they will all sing along to, entirely in the wrong key and at least two syllables behind the actual song, and then a shaven-headed hardman who will attempt to bring proceedings under control by programming the box to play 'Live Forever' by Oasis seventeen times in a row.

K

KALE

Green or purple leafed vegetable, the cultivation of which was encouraged in Britain during the Second World War on the grounds that it was affordable and easy to grow at home. True fact! Unfortunately, due to an oversight, once the war was over the government forgot to admit that kale was actually quite disgusting and no one should bother eating it ever again.

KEEGAN, KEVIN

A national hero in Britain, not so much for his football playing per se but because he looked exactly like everyone thought a 1970s footballer should. That is to say, permed and reeking of Brut.

KEMP, ROSS

Spherical-headed British actor famed for his whispering role in *EastEnders* and for prowling the world whispering about gangs. Unfortunately, in 2009 Jeremy Clarkson foolishly used Kemp to demonstrate the luggage capacity of a Renault Twingo and then forgot to get him out of the boot again before crashing headlong into the icy waters of Belfast docks. After years of whispering about things, Kemp was unable to remember how to shout for help and remains down there to this day, suckling air out of the spare wheel well. At least we assume so. You don't see him on telly so much so that's almost certainly what happened.

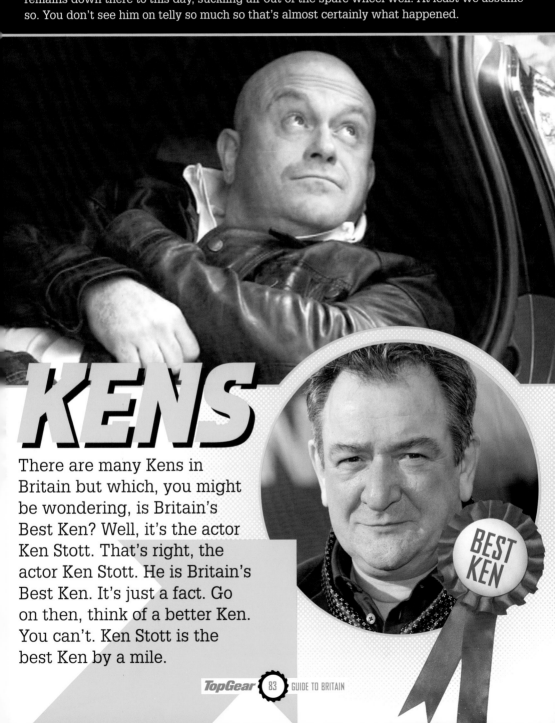

KENS

There are many Kens in Britain but which, you might be wondering, is Britain's Best Ken? Well, it's the actor Ken Stott. That's right, the actor Ken Stott. He is Britain's Best Ken. It's just a fact. Go on then, think of a better Ken. You can't. Ken Stott is the best Ken by a mile.

BEST KEN

KICKING THINGS

The British love kicking things. Indeed, most British sport is basically about kicking things. Football; kicking things. Rugby; running about a bit then kicking things. Cricket; not about kicking things. Which is probably why it's so boring.

KILTS

Traditional Scottish men's trouser substitute now sported almost exclusively by music students earning a few quid by playing bagpipes outside Edinburgh landmarks and ex-pat Scottish people attending weddings in England. The latter do this for two reasons. First of all, because they can and because they think that doing so will give them a good excuse to talk to all the bride's single friends. And secondly, because there's nothing the Scottish like more than making the English feel faintly uneasy with the thought that at any second a Scotman could effortlessly show them his arse.

KIT CARS

There is a segment of the British population that thinks, 'I do not want a car made by Ford or Vauxhall or Renault or any of the other large corporations who have made it their business to design and assemble cars to a high standard perfected over many decades. No, what I want is a car that I, Nigel Philpott, a loss-adjuster and in no way an automotive engineer, have built myself in my garage. Oh yes, there is no doubt in my mind that this will be vastly superior to the efforts of these so-called car manufacturers.' Unfortunately, Mr Philpott will then spend seven years of his life skinning his knuckles to assemble a ghastly sports car with the suspension of a Morris Ital and the appearance of a collapsed canoe or a crude lookalike that aims to pass itself off as a Lamborghini yet would fail to fool even someone who had never seen a real Lamborghini. A few years ago, the kit car industry tried to make itself seem more professional and grown up by insisting that its products were referred to as 'component cars'. What they really should be called, however, is 'divorce makers'.

KNIGHTHOODS

To receive a knighthood is to be summoned to Buckingham Palace, where Her Majesty the Queen will waft a sword about your head and then engage you in precisely 47 seconds of small talk about where you are from. Little wonder that it is the ultimate honour a British man can receive. In fact, the percentage of knighted people who actively use their knighthood is surprisingly small. Sir Elton John, for example, has never once leapt onto a large white horse and ridden into the uncharted lands to slay some dragons. At least, not that we know of. Most British knights of modern times prefer to keep their knighthoods hidden. Largely, this is down to natural British reticence, and also because it's a complete faff getting all your bank cards changed.

KNOCKERS

A uniquely British word for breasts, still in use alongside other quintessentially British words for breasts such as jubblies and Bristols. From this we can conclude that the British have a weirdly large number of word for breasts.

LAND ROVER

Midlands-based 4x4 maker enjoying considerable success across the globe with its range of highly desirable products. However, despite this global triumph there are plenty of people in Britain who believe that a true Land Rover is not a smart and sophisticated SUV and should be a creaky green lump of dented ally, canvas and moss which will consume all of your spare time as you attempt to prevent it letting water in and oil out with little success at either.

LEAVES

Small pieces of foliage which in summer makes trees look nice and in autumn make the entire British railway network grind to a halt.

LIBRARY, THE BRITISH

The national library of Britain and a vast archive of printed matter stretching back many centuries, making it one of the largest libraries in the entire world. Unfortunately, the British Library building itself inadvertently resembles a large branch of Tesco and is regular confused with one, leading to all manner of confusions ranging from people believing the last Harry Potter book was 'a bit yoghurty' to several portions of extremely papery spag bol.

HARRY POTTER
and the Peach Melba Yogurt of Doom

LIVERPOOL

A North Western maritime city with a great tradition of creativity in the arts, music and sport. Over the years many great entertainers have come from Liverpool, from Cilla Black and Paul McCartney to Stan Boardman and Carla Lane. To this day, proud celebrity Scousers such as these meet to talk about how great Liverpool is in their favourite local, the Red Lion in Cookham, Berkshire.

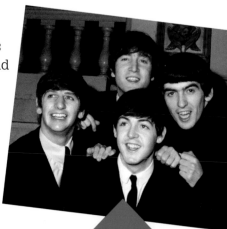

Some Liverpudlians

TOP FACT

The Beatles were from Liverpool but don't worry, no one from Liverpool ever mentions this.

LOCAL RADIO DJs

Local radio is an important part of British broadcasting and gives vital employment to people who like pronounce their Ts as Ds, have no qualms about driving around in a free car with their own name on the side and like to sit in a room on their own making light chit-chat into a foam bulb before announcing a Tina Turner record.
See also; Americans, British people who speak like.

LOCK-IN, THE

A great British tradition in which a pub landlord will, for a select few customers, bolt the doors of his establishment and carry on serving drinks long after the usual 11pm closing time. The start of a lock-in can be identified by the gentle but persistent removal of those drinkers who are not going to be invited to join in, followed by the discreet drawing of the pub curtains to avoid detection by the police. Unless you are in the countryside, in which case the entire local police force is already inside the pub and he too wants another pint. A lock-in is one of the most thrilling things a British person can get involved in for three simple reasons. Firstly, there's the sense of breaking the law, even if it's in a very casual and consequence-free way. Secondly, to be allowed to stay in the pub as lock-in breaks out suggests a bond of trust between you and the landlord. And thirdly, because it means you can have another drink.

LONDON

Capital of England and the United Kingdom and often regarded as one of the greatest cities in the entire world, a view that is widely rejected by the rest of Britain who like to regard it with resentment, suspicion and a half-remembered anecdote from someone's cousin about a friend-of-a-friend who was literally robbed at knifepoint in the toiletries aisle of a supermarket on Tottenham Court Road. Of course, the people of almost every country in the world hold such wildly distorted and cynical views of their own capital which is why, for example, the French believe that Paris is full of extremely rude people trying to rip you off even though that is... oh, hang on.

LONDON STANSTED

'London' Stansted airport isn't just conspicuously not in London but actually a good 30 miles from it, halfway up Essex. Ergo, one of the biggest fibs in international travel. See also 'London Oxford Airport'. You've got Oxford in your name. Just enjoy that and stop being greedy.

London.

Not London.

LOTUS

Norfolk-based maker of excellent lightweight sports cars. Recently fell under the control of a man called Dany Bahar who decided that they shouldn't be a maker of excellent lightweight sports cars and announced five brand new models all at the same time, even though none of them was actually ready, and then spent a lot of time hiring American rappers as consultants and publishing 'lifestyle' magazines so glossy it was like trying to read a block of condensed milk rather than cracking on with anything useful. Fortunately, Lotus got tired of his drivel and let him go before announcing that they were going to carry on being a maker of excellent lightweight sports cars. So, erm, as you were.

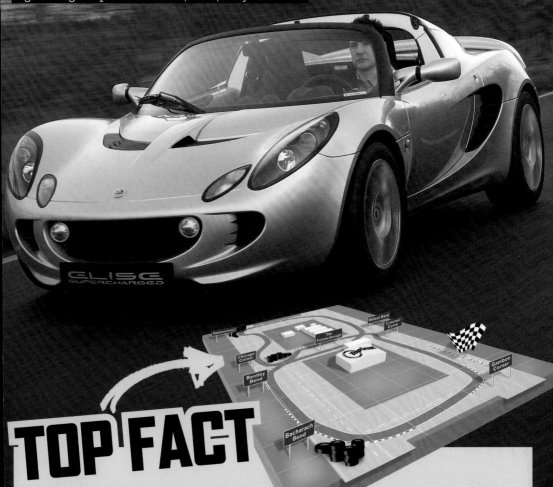

TOP FACT

Sections of the *Top Gear* test track were designed by the crack chassis team from Lotus in order to smoke out poor handling characteristics in a range of cars. Rumours that during Dany Bahar's reign they wanted to come back and redesign the track to make it heavier and worse are unfounded.

M MANCHESTER

Proud industrial city of the North West and technically England's third city, although Manchester spends a great deal of time and energy trying to prove that it doesn't care about such things because it is better than London and Birmingham put together. If a city can be personified by one person, Manchester is encapsulated in the cocky, no-messing confidence of former Oasis frontman Liam Gallagher. Although Manchester itself isn't a swaggering tit in a parka.

TOP FACT

Manchester is famed for its high levels of rainfall, although this can be exaggerated. The rain does stop, often for up to 28 minutes per month (in the summer).

MARKS & SPENCER

Bedrock of the British high street and the place from which literally everyone in Britain buys their socks. Unless you are Jeremy Clarkson, in which case you claim never to have been into a Marks & Spencer in your life, an act which is basically tantamount to treason.

MARMALADE

Fruity preserve, usually orange-based, which is a significant breakfast-time staple and would attract considerable disgust from a British person if eaten at any other time of day. The British like orange marmalade first thing in the morning because they can pretend it counts as one of their five-a-day.

MARMITE

Polarising and quintessentially British savoury spread made from an unwanted by-product of the beer-brewing process which other nations would throw away. The fact that the British like to eat it demonstrates a classic British quality - resourcefulness. And willingness to eat something that looks and tastes like the contents of a smoker's lungs.

MATE

Chummy way for British men to refer to other men and used with great relish, firstly because it enables you to converse with a person whose name you have completely forgotten, and secondly, because it allows you to feel slightly more at ease when talking to a plumber.

McLAREN

Leading British F1 team. Also makers of the legendary F1 road car and, more recently, the very excellent 12C supercar. Run by the legendarily obsessive Ron Dennis, a man so fastidious that he probably thinks operating theatres are 'grubby'.

METRIFICATION

Many countries around the world cheerfully embrace the simple logic of the metric system. The United States, on the other hand, staunchly resists such a move and its people still refer to faithful miles, feet and inches in everyday life. Britain does neither. What Britain prefers is a cunning and seemingly quite random mixture of both. In British schools, children are taught to measure in centimetres, yet British speed limits are expressed in miles per hour. By extension, British time is written out as am or pm and not in fancy European 24 hour format, yet temperatures are increasingly dispensed in modern centigrade (thought the TV weatherman will often give the same reading in Fahrenheit as well, just to be on the safe side). To an outside observer this strange mixture of old and new might seem shambolic and absurd yet in fact it is carefully considered and represents two things the British enjoy very much; 1. Respecting tradition. 2. Confusing foreigners.

METRE

Standard metric unit of measurement equivalent to 100 centimetres. Since Britain began to adopt the metric system in the mid-1960s, expressing distance or height in metres should be perfectly acceptable. However, in many circles to use the word 'metres' in Britain is still to make yourself sound a bit suspicious, especially since 'yards' is basically the same thing.

A Yard

A Metre

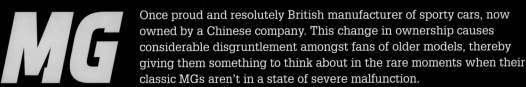

MG

Once proud and resolutely British manufacturer of sporty cars, now owned by a Chinese company. This change in ownership causes considerable disgruntlement amongst fans of older models, thereby giving them something to think about in the rare moments when their classic MGs aren't in a state of severe malfunction.

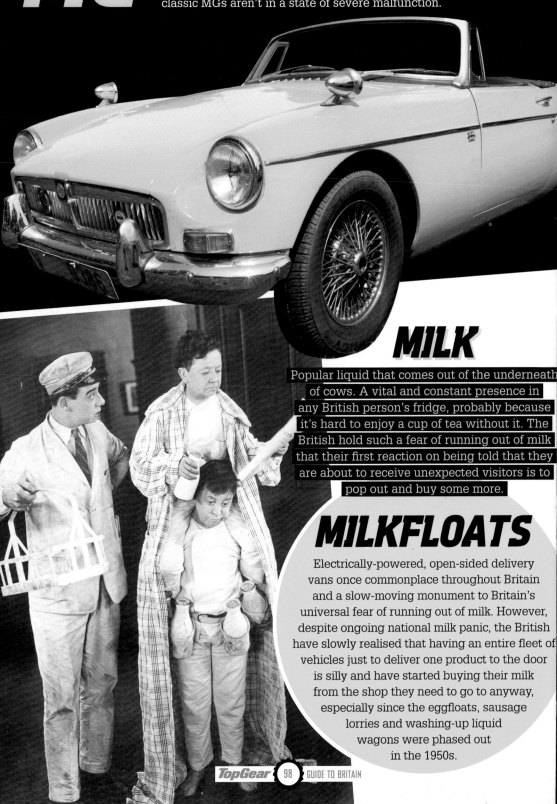

MILK

Popular liquid that comes out of the underneath of cows. A vital and constant presence in any British person's fridge, probably because it's hard to enjoy a cup of tea without it. The British hold such a fear of running out of milk that their first reaction on being told that they are about to receive unexpected visitors is to pop out and buy some more.

MILKFLOATS

Electrically-powered, open-sided delivery vans once commonplace throughout Britain and a slow-moving monument to Britain's universal fear of running out of milk. However, despite ongoing national milk panic, the British have slowly realised that having an entire fleet of vehicles just to deliver one product to the door is silly and have started buying their milk from the shop they need to go to anyway, especially since the eggfloats, sausage lorries and washing-up liquid wagons were phased out in the 1950s.

MINI (OLD)

Tiny car originally designed as sensible, economical transport but successfully hijacked by groovy folk in fur waistcoats and adventurous trousers to become a 1960s icon and an enduring staple of any British street scene until 2000 when production finally ceased. A very popular car but not a very rustproof one, which is why many Minis perished and those that are left now appear on eBay with a starting price of squifty bajillion pounds even though all the lights are smashed, the seats are missing and the body seems to have been resprayed with a hammer.

TOP FACT

The sporty Mini Cooper gets its name from John Cooper, one of the first people to tune the original Mini back in the 1960s. This model probably wouldn't be so appealing if his name had been John Sidebottom. Or John Manlove.

MINI (NEW)

Modern recreation of the old Mini trading on the swinging sixties image but without the oil leaks and strange smell of damp. Comes in two basic flavours; the normal hatchback, which is excellent and built in Oxford, and the super-sized Countryman, which is not. Mini may sound quintessentially British but the company is now part of BMW, a fact which causes considerable harrumphing across Britain.

MINICAB

A popular way for British people to get around, especially if they want to have a sinking feeling that they're not actually going in the right direction. Minicabs typically differ from normal cabs in several important ways. First of all, they should always smell of a powerful air freshener, one which emits a not-very-nice fragrance that is clearly masking an even worse smell. Secondly, they should have at least one unsettling sticky patch on the back seat which is only discovered when the occupant inadvertently puts their hand on it. And finally, they should at all times have at least one troubling warning light illuminated on the dashboard, usually the little yellow one labelled 'check engine'. This is true even of that ever-popular minicab staple, the Skoda Octavia, which really does have a Czech engine.

PUNGENT CARS
We'll get you there probably!

We can take you to:
Near your home!
Somewhere that looks like your office!
An airport!

Just call 0800-WORRYINGSUSPENSIONNOISE

MOANING

The British like nothing more than a good moan on a whole range of subjects from bad backs and the price of petrol to government policies and things they've seen on *Top Gear*. Most of all, the British like to moan about the weather, even if to most reasoned eyes the weather is actually quite nice. Hence why during the hot spell in summer 2013 a BBC weathercaster actually said to viewers, 'It's going to be hot again tomorrow, I'm afraid'.

MORGAN

Malvern-based maker of quirky old-fashioned sports cars, mostly to a design first sketched out when no one had mains electricity. As a consequence, Morgans are still built around a wooden frame although they have made certain nods to modernity such as indicators that flash rather than pop out of the sides, and the deletion of the dashboard-mounted monocle holder. Most radically, some models now use engines made by the perfidious Jerries at BMW, much to the dismay of many Morgan employees who still rush out of the factory every day in the hope of being able to salute a passing Spitfire.

MORRIS DANCING

Much maligned type of folk performance unfairly seen as the kind of thing invented solely to ruin a rural fete or beer festival. In fact, Morris dancing was originally developed as a way of defending Great Britain against foreign attack. Upon sighting unfriendly ships off the British coast, the Morris men would assemble atop a nearby cliff and begin their complex, prancing routine of bell-rattling and stick-bashing thereby causing the overseas aggressors to think, 'Oh my God, Britain looks like a bloody awful place' and turn their ships around immediately.

MOTORWAY SERVICE STATIONS

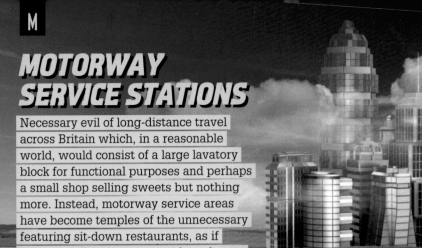

Necessary evil of long-distance travel across Britain which, in a reasonable world, would consist of a large lavatory block for functional purposes and perhaps a small shop selling sweets but nothing more. Instead, motorway service areas have become temples of the unnecessary featuring sit-down restaurants, as if anyone really wants to spend any longer there than they have to, and shops that sell clothes, as if anyone embarks on a long journey and then realises that they've forgotten to put on their trousers. The real and unsung flaw in motorway service stations, however, is that due to some arcane combination of poor lighting, poor layout and the constant whiff of despair in the air, they are capable of making everyone in them look miserable and unattractive.

MURRAY, ANDY

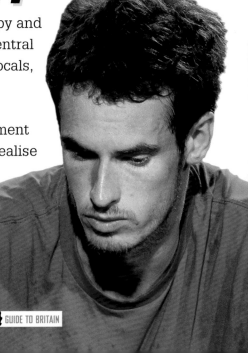

Scottish tennis player regarded as grumpy and untalkative, except in his homeland of central Scotland where, in comparison to most locals, he is a cheery chatterbox. Murray finally realised a dream when he won the 2013 Wimbledon men's final and this achievement was all the more remarkable when you realise that the temperature on centre court was reported as 50°C or precisely five times the maximum operating temperature of a Scotsman.

MUSIC HALL

Once-popular British theatrical entertainment in which a Cockney man would make quips about a country we had recently engaged in war, a woman with very tall hair would sing in a very high voice, and another gentlemen would play a kind of musical instrument which no longer exists. Killed off by television and, from the sound of it, not a moment too soon.

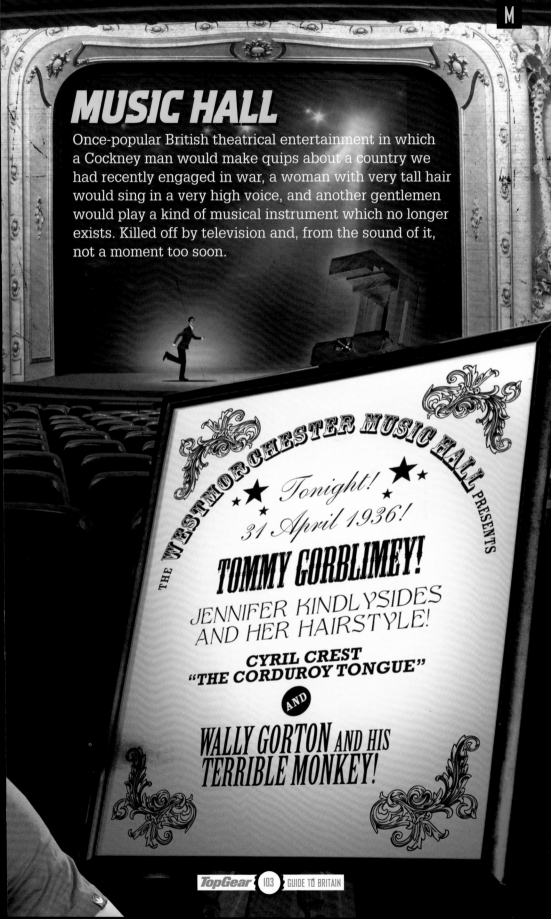

THE WESTMORCHESTER MUSIC HALL PRESENTS

★ ★ *Tonight!* ★ ★
31 April 1936!

TOMMY GORBLIMEY!

JENNIFER KINDLYSIDES AND HER HAIRSTYLE!

CYRIL CREST "THE CORDUROY TONGUE"

AND

WALLY GORTON AND HIS TERRIBLE MONKEY!

NATIONAL TRUST, THE

Charity chiefly concerned with the preservation of old buildings so that they can be visited by old people, often in a car which demonstrates how much the occupants like the National Trust by having a National Trust sticker in the back window. While it's all very nice to go and look at well-preserved old stuff and, when they've got out of the way, the neoclassical manor house they're wandering around, the chief downside of National Trust properties is the tea shop. Specifically, it is the smell of the tea shop, a sort of dull, cakey fug that gets onto your clothes and which you'll be smelling all the way home. It is a smell that exists nowhere else and which would be instantly recognisable if it were bottled and sold as Eau Du National Trust Tea Shop. Except no one would buy such a thing because, as a smell, it's basically disgusting. And anyway, as we've established, if you wanted to smell like that you could just go and hang out in an actual National Trust tea shop for 20 minutes.

NEWS, THE

Televisual summary of national and global current events. Even in an age of the internet, TV on-demand and rolling news channels, the British still like the stout reassurance of bulletins on the telly at pre-ordained times, those times typically being 1pm, 6pm and 10pm. Many British people can peg their daily routines to this, especially if they are old. So if you're thinking of burgling a British person over the age of 60, just wait until the 10 o'clock news is over. They're bound to go to bed immediately afterwards. Just remember to allow an extra three or four minutes after the actual news for them to watch the weather forecast.

NEWSPAPERS

Formerly a politically and tonally varied source of information about current affairs that more recently decided to start hacking telephones and acting like a division of MI5, but one concerned with finding out if Sienna Miller has got any pants on.

Twatface Jenkins	7946 0025
Arsebreath	7946 0215
Big Ears O'Reilly	0118 496 0001
Smelly McBurger	7946 0687
Weaselsticks	7946 0152
The Chunky Biscuit	7946 0562
Salad Boy	7946 0871
James May	0118 496 0084

NICKNAMES

British men are great fans of giving their friends nicknames. To people from other countries this can sometimes seem confusing when, for example, a chap's best friend from childhood, his ally, his consort, his confidant, the best man at his wedding and the godfather to his first born child is still cheerfully referred to as 'Twatface'.

NOBLE

Plucky British supercar maker more than capable of giving the big boys a bloody nose. Yes, Ferrari might have their years of Formula 1 experience and their legendary Maranello factory but don't forget, Noble has a way of getting 650 horsepower from a Volvo engine and a medium-sized industrial unit near Leicester.

NORFOLK

County in eastern England famed for mustard, Lotus and Alan Partridge. Norfolk is often unfairly portrayed as a hot-bed of inbreeding, something that upsets the local residents who will respond to such accusations by rolling at least two of their eyes.

NOISINESS

Being noisy is an extremely un-British thing. In fact, if you ask a British person what they dislike about, say, the Greeks or the Spanish, it is quite likely that the answer will be 'noisiness'. Or their lavatories.

NOTICE BOARDS

A required part of any British village scene, the rural notice board is cleverly designed so that from a distance it looks enticing and interesting and it is only upon closer inspection it reveals itself to be full of troublingly handwritten signs about 'yogar clases' and is in fact staggeringly dull.

O

OAVES

The plural of 'oaf'. Or at least it should be.

See also; idiots

OLYMPICS, THE

The London 2012 Olympics were generally acknowledged to be a huge success and a triumph of British creativity and organisation which made everyone in the country extremely proud. This event was a very telling reflection of the British character, not because they were very well hosted but because before they started everyone in Britain assumed we were going to cock them up.

LONDON 2012
AMBITIOUS
BUT
RUBBISH

ONE DIRECTION

British boy band apparently 'cracking' the United States. Despite the name, this ensemble actually has several directions otherwise they'd all be stuck in a corner. Sadly, none of the directions has yet turned out to be 'directly into an industrial mincing machine'.

ONE-WAY SYSTEMS

Mono-directional traffic flow systems ostensibly designed to smooth the passage of cars, vans and lorries, often through streets that were built before the advent of internal combustion and are therefore narrower than might be desirable. Actually none of that is true. One-way systems are there purely to annoy, confuse and, in the case of many British towns, ensure that no matter what you do, you will always end up at the railway station.

OTTERS

Semi-aquatic river-centric mammals found throughout Britain, otters are contractually obliged to appear as the subject of an item at least once during every series of *Countryfile*.

NOT ACTUALLY OVAL

OVAL

A station on the London Underground. 'This station is Oval' says the announcement on the trains. But it isn't.

PAGE 3

Quaint British tradition in which the nation's best-selling newspapers proudly depict a daily pair of breasts immediately inside as if it's 1973 and everyone goes to work in a brown suit to drink Scotch at their desk. The continuing existence of Page 3 even though it isn't 1973 is probably one of those things that makes foreigners think the British are a bit odd. Obviously, not the French or the Italians. You can't turn on a TV in France or Italy without seeing a pair of naked boobs, even if the programme you're watching turns out to be their version of *Question Time* and the naked boobs belong to the Minister for Education & Regional Development. However, the rest of the world finds all this strange and about 40 years out of date. There is much debate in Britain about the continued existence of Page 3. Opponents say it is sexist, demeaning and outdated. This is a very valid argument. In the opposite camp is one over-riding fact; men quite like looking at boobs.

PANCAKE DAY

The French dander around all year long eating crêpes to their heart's content yet the British steadfastly refuse to eat pancakes with any gusto unless it is Pancake Day. A British person might have all the necessary ingredients to make pancakes and be consumed by a terrible craving for pancakes, but they simply cannot prepare or consume pancakes unless it is actually Pancake Day. In most British households this is not a religious thing, it is simply the rules. Pancake Day therefore illustrates the great British desire to respect tradition, even if the tradition is bloody-mindedly idiotic.

PANTOMIME

Unique British theatrical tradition based around men dressed as women and audience participation re. repeated low-level disagreement and things being behind members of the cast. Pantomime is a key reason why people from other countries thinking the British are strange.

PEARLY KINGS

British tradition emanating from, and still largely limited to, the East End of London. Pearly kings (and their pearly queen companions) like nothing more than telling you how proud they are to be East Enders because the East End is the best place in the world. In truth their opinions are useless because they have never been anywhere *except* the East End on account of their button-covered clothing which renders even short car journeys intolerably uncomfortable and sends airport metal detectors into meltdown.

PERIOD DRAMA

Many countries have a fine tradition of performance art yet only Britain has managed to carve a niche built entirely upon old country houses and being able to use them as locations for films and TV series in which handsome but mysterious men ride around on horses looking rugged and fey girls in enormous dresses clutch small lacy handkerchiefs and then swoon onto a chaise longue. Generally unappealing to men on account of rarely containing a car chase.

THEIRS WAS A LOVE THAT COULD NEVER GET PAST THE SIMPLY
INCREDIBLE NUMBER OF ANTI-MACASSARS IN HER HOUSE

GIN & GENTILITY

KEIRA KNIGHTLEY

COLIN FIRTH

JUDI DENCH IN A BUSTLE

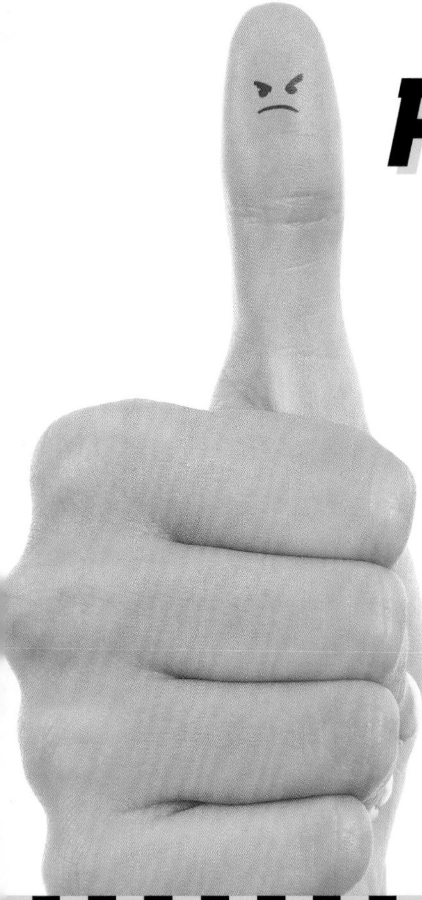

PICKLES, ERIC

Almost spherical Northern man current serving as minister for something-or-other in the government, notable chiefly for having a very, very big head but a very, very small face. As a result, you can make your own Eric Pickles at home by the simple act of drawing a tiny face on your own thumb. Although of course this may lead to your thumb being appointed Secretary of State for Communities & Local Government.

PIES

Ingenious food stuff based around the simple premise that everything tastes better when it's encased in pastry. The staple diet of James May.

Full English breakfast pie
Mars bar pie
Pint of milk pie
Blu-ray boxset of the Jason Bourne films pie
Distracting sense of wistfulness pie
Pie pie

MAY'S BAKERY

PIKE, DON'T TELL HIM

A famous line from the sit-com *Dad's Army* and possibly the funniest thing many British people have heard in their lives. This is not only because it's an excellent joke relayed by an excellent comic actor, but also because it involves the war. Ergo, a perfect storm of British amusement.

PILOTS

To be a British airline pilot you must have three qualities. Firstly, a single syllable name such as Mike, John or Rob. Secondly, a very smooth voice with a just a trace of a mid-Atlantic soft T sound. And finally, a slightly unusual way of saying 'Errrr' between sentences which sounds strangely reassuring, sort of like you're sucking in a purr. Oh, and if you're any good at making a plane take off and land then all the better. But mainly the first three things.

PINTS

A standard measurement for liquid under the imperial system. Also the standard quantity in which British beer is dispensed in pubs. If you asked a European person to join you in a bar where you intended to consume almost two-and-a-half litres of beer in quick succession they would probably think you were a lunatic. Unless perhaps they were German. However, when a British person invites a friend or colleague to the pub 'for a quick couple of pints' (which will invariably see the consumption of at least four pints) this is considered normal even though, rationally speaking, that's quite a lot of liquid to see away in one sitting. In newspapers and parliament it is sometimes asked why the British drink so much alcohol. Strangely, no one ever alights on the real answer, which is because the British are good at it.
See also; beer; quick pint, a.

British

European. Drink up.

PLOUGHMAN'S LUNCH

British lunchtime staple often served in pubs and consisting of a hunk of bread, a lump of cheese and a pickled onion, perhaps with some cold ham on the side. Basically it's just a random grab bag of things that can be pulled from the fridge and bunged on a plate with absolutely no effort whatsoever on the part of whoever's cooking. The traditional job of ploughman has died out in Britain and, based on what they got for lunch, it's quite clear why: it was bloody miserable.

P

POPMASTER

A popular mid-morning music quiz during the Ken Bruce show on BBC Radio 2. Notable firstly because it's fun to play along with and secondly because every single contestant who is asked to guess the year from a series of musical clues will always, without fail, give an answer that is one year out.

POPPING

In Britain the act of 'popping' can only be used in one context: To describe a very quick trip to the shops in order to buy, at most, three items. What's interesting about 'popping' to the shops is that it has no literal translation in any other language. Probably. In fairness, we haven't checked. But it seems unlikely. If they do have the word 'popping' in German it almost certainly means something mucky.

PORNOGRAPHY

There are many nations that have nurtured a thriving pornography industry. Sweden, for example. Or the United States. Great Britain is not one of those nations. This is not because of any great moral objection but simply because there is no demand for porn films in which the protagonists start with a lengthy discussion about the weather.

TopGear 118 GUIDE TO BRITAIN

POSH POPSTARS

As part of Britain's dedication to inverted snobbery, British pop and rock stars are generally given greater respect if they claim to come from an extremely humble and poverty-stricken background. It's why John Lennon studiously styled himself as a working-class hero even though he grew up in a suburban semi. Conversely, if musicians are well-spoken and appear to be unfazed by which fork to use at a very formal dinner, they are treated with thinly-veiled distain. Which is one of the reasons why it's fashionable to say that Mumford & Sons are shite.

NME

EXCLUSIVE!

GIVING US AN ART ATTACK

BRIAN SEWELL'S NEW ALBUM REVIEWED IN FULL

Spoiler alert! He's a posh git and it's rubbish

Royal Fail

Sorry, we haven't delivered.

Today's date

Time

Name

Address   Postcode

Reason for not delivering

☐ We couldn't be bothered to knock

☐ You were probably in the shower

☐ Your front door looked too far away so we gave up

☐ We thought we heard a dog and decided to just go back to the depot

because

☐ a signature is required

☐ It's too big for your letterbox

Please see overleaf for information on where your item is now.

Item number

Delivery person duty number

POST OFFICE, THE

Ailing national delivery service, once tasked with shepherding written communications across Britain. Unfortunately for them, e-mail came along and ruined everything, which means these days the main business of the Post Office is to put notes through your door telling you that they tried to deliver a package. Under the unwritten laws of Britain, actually getting hold of your package is not the direct responsibility of the Post Office and requires you to set aside three working days in order to queue up in the sorting office, during which time you might seriously consider writing off the cost of the DVD you ordered from Amazon and trudging home to weep silently into the small, red Post Office branded card that heralded the start of this whole fiasco in the first place.

POTHOLES

Holes in a road surface and now so massive and widespread that, technically speaking, 37 percent of Britain is currently below sea level.

FREE HOUSE

The QUEEN VICTORIA

PRINCESS ANNE
See Reliant Scimitar

THE QUEEN VICTORIA

Free House

Homecooked **LUNCHES**

Ales on Handpumps

THE QUEEN VICTORIA

Wines & **SPIRITS**

Traditional **ALES**

PUBS

The bedrock of British life, especially the slightly dated depiction of British life in soap operas. The pub is distinct from the bar for a number of reasons. First of all, bars often offer table service whereas pubs make you work for your drink by getting up to fetch it. Secondly, bars major on wines and light lagers whereas the best drinks to consume in a pub are classically British ones. In other words, anything tepid and brown. Thirdly, the décor of a bar can be minimalist and clever whereas a pub should be decorated in a manner that reflects the drinks it serves. Again, tepid and brown. Sadly, many British pubs were ruined by the smoking ban as it turned out that the smell of stale smoke was masking the even worse stench of beer, sweat and farts.

QUEEN, THE

Constitutional head of the United Kingdom and the Commonwealth. It is said that everywhere the Queen goes will be spruced up prior to her arrival and that, as a result, the Queen thinks the whole world smells of paint. Extending this theme, it's possible that the Queen also thinks the whole world is covered in bunting, that it's infested with moderately inept primary school bands, and that its entire population has really sweaty hands. As a result, being the Queen is basically a living nightmare.

QUEUES LIKELY

Warning! Bloody Obvious Being Stated Ahead

Ominous and defeatist road sign erected at precisely the point where a driver will already be stuck in the predicted traffic jam and can therefore do absolutely nothing whatsoever with the depressing information provided. Presumably invented by the same person who thought of putting 'WARNING: FOG' on those dot matrix boards above motorways in case anyone mistakenly thought the dense white mist in the air meant they had crashed into an enormous marshmallow.

QUICK PINT, A

Noble British tradition in which two or more colleagues will go to a pub after work for what is billed, with all good intentions, as an endeavour of limited time and quantity. Seven hours later when all parties concerned are falling out of an Indian restaurant, nightclub or lock-in the 'quick pint' will be adjudged a great success, especially for a Monday evening.

QUIZZES

The British love a quiz, especially if it gives them the chance to look slightly more intelligent than other people. The most popular type of quiz is the pub quiz, although these are unfortunately very hard to win thanks to the constant presence of a team of four bearded men in extremely beige clothes who will win every round, even ones entitled 'types of giraffe' or 'the works of Miley Cyrus', without the apparent need for one of them to nip off to the loo and look up the tricky bits on their mobile phone.

R

RALEIGH CHOPPER

Giddily wobbly children's bicycle boasting a massive back wheel and a smaller front one, enormously tall handlebars and a testicle-threatening central gear shifter. Remembered with great fondness as literally the most 1970s thing British people of a certain age have ever owned, which is fine unless those people of a certain age are very minor celebrities and are on a programme about the 1970s sharing their tissue-thin observations about a decade which ended when they were about seven.

RALEIGH, SIR WALTER

An under-rated British hero, not because he discovered tobacco and the potato but because he *didn't* discover tobacco and the potato yet *claimed* he did in order to impress a girl. Although in this case the girl was Queen Elizabeth and it didn't work out so well in the end.

RECUMBENT BICYCLES

Idiotic and needless variation on the basic idea of the bicycle that seems to be less comfortable, less stable and less able to be seen by drivers of cars, lorries and other things that might easily crush it under their wheels. Ergo, has no apparent benefits over a normal bicycle apart from telling the world that you are a nerdish, contrary, attention-seeking, lycra-clad tit.

R
RELIANT KITTEN

Sister car to the Reliant Robin (see below), the Kitten was identical in many respects including the engine, the interior and the basic style of the body. There was just one small but rather significant difference: It had four wheels. The Kitten was therefore like a Robin but did not fall over. Although, disappointingly given its name, it still wasn't capable of running up the curtains.

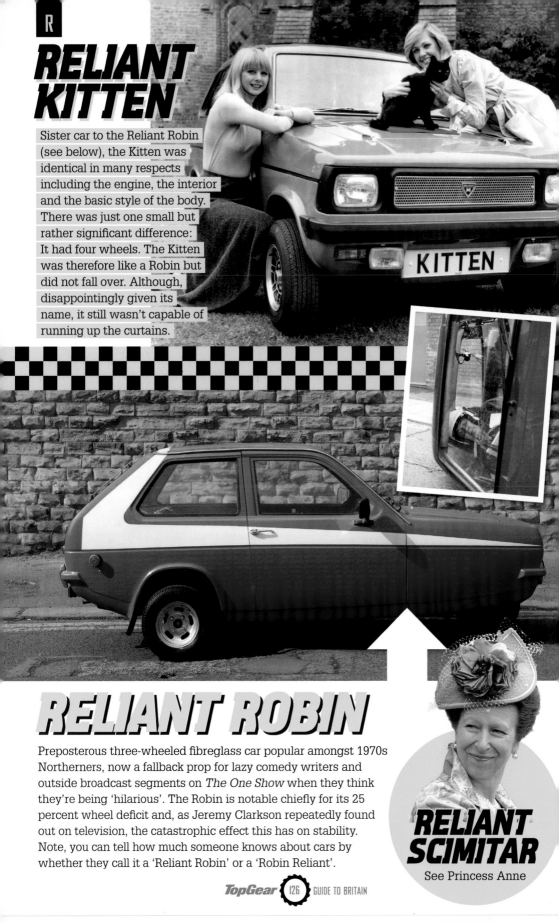

RELIANT ROBIN

Preposterous three-wheeled fibreglass car popular amongst 1970s Northerners, now a fallback prop for lazy comedy writers and outside broadcast segments on *The One Show* when they think they're being 'hilarious'. The Robin is notable chiefly for its 25 percent wheel deficit and, as Jeremy Clarkson repeatedly found out on television, the catastrophic effect this has on stability. Note, you can tell how much someone knows about cars by whether they call it a 'Reliant Robin' or a 'Robin Reliant'.

RELIANT SCIMITAR

See Princess Anne

RHYMING SLANG

A great British tradition and especially popular amongst Cockneys. In fact, the only things a Cockney likes more than rhyming slang is a sing-song or an opportunity to point at their street and tell you it was bombed during the war. Or, as they might pronounce it, 'the woo-uh'. Unfortunately, rhyming slang is completely rubbish and cannot be used in a normal conversation. As such, rhyming slang's main use is as part of a general British mission to stop foreigners knowing what the bloody hell they're talking about.

LESSER KNOWN RHYMING SLANG

Rodney Bewes – *shoes*

Great Aunt Bess – *cress*

James May – *A brownish shade of grey*

Dame Judi Dench – *park bench*

Lucky guess - *cress*

Park bench – *Dame Judi Dench*

Richard Hammond – *smoked salmon*

Eton Mess – *cress*

Telephone banking call centre – *polenta*

Rudolf Hess – *cress*

Jeremy Clarkson – *Hammer*

ROAST POTATOES

Oven-cooked staple and the perfect accompaniment to a joint of meat, consumed with glee by British people, especially on a Sunday. The main thing to note about roast potatoes is that everyone in Britain thinks they can cook them better than absolutely anyone else in the country.

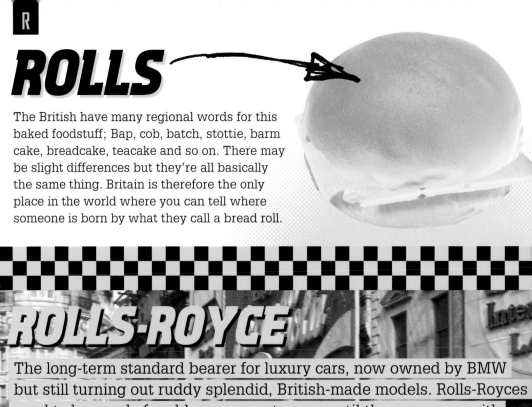

R

ROLLS

The British have many regional words for this baked foodstuff; Bap, cob, batch, stottie, barm cake, breadcake, teacake and so on. There may be slight differences but they're all basically the same thing. Britain is therefore the only place in the world where you can tell where someone is born by what they call a bread roll.

ROLLS-ROYCE

The long-term standard bearer for luxury cars, now owned by BMW but still turning out ruddy splendid, British-made models. Rolls-Royces used to be purely for old-money customers until they came up with the Silver Shadow model of the 1960s which was smaller and more affordable, becoming the car of choice for successful light entertainers through the 1960s and 1970s. These cars can be picked up for a song these days, assuming they haven't recently been impounded by the police as evidence.

ROOOOOOONEEEEEY!

The single most moronic thing a British person can say. Especially if Wayne Rooney is not playing football in front of you and you're actually in the reading room of the British Library.

ROVER

Once-proud maker of quiet and restrained quality cars for stout sensible people like bank managers and civil servants. Utterly derailed after absorption into the corporate mush of British Leyland, marking a slow decline through innovative designs that didn't work properly and gussied-up Hondas which did work properly but weren't very interesting. Reached a low point in the 2000s when the formerly illustrious name was crudely gummed to a low-rent Indian hatchback and sold as the CityRover which turned out to be the worst car in the history of the world. Company collapsed soon afterwards. The name is now owned by Jaguar Land Rover who, perhaps wisely, keep it locked in a cupboard and don't let anyone touch it.

RUDENESS

On the one hand, the British are incredibly tolerant of rudeness, which is why a British waiter could openly gob in their soup and still expect to receive a small tip. On the other hand, the British cannot abide rudeness outside of shop or restaurant staff, and almost nothing will cause a pursing of the lips and an agitated conversation in the car on the way home like a perceived piece of rude behaviour at a social gathering. One of the single most chilling things a British person can hear is someone else saying, 'How rude!' in contrast to certain other European countries, where this is a remark of admiration.

RUDENESS, COVERT

WITH THE GREATEST RESPECT...

Although the British hate rudeness (see above) they have developed several clever ways of being able to say something rude by first softening the blow. The technique is extremely straightforward and simply requires you to prefix whatever it is you're about to say with a phrase such as 'with the greatest respect' or 'no offence, but...'. Hey presto, you've then got free reign to call someone an arse, laugh at their curtains or tell them that their fruitcake tastes of cat.

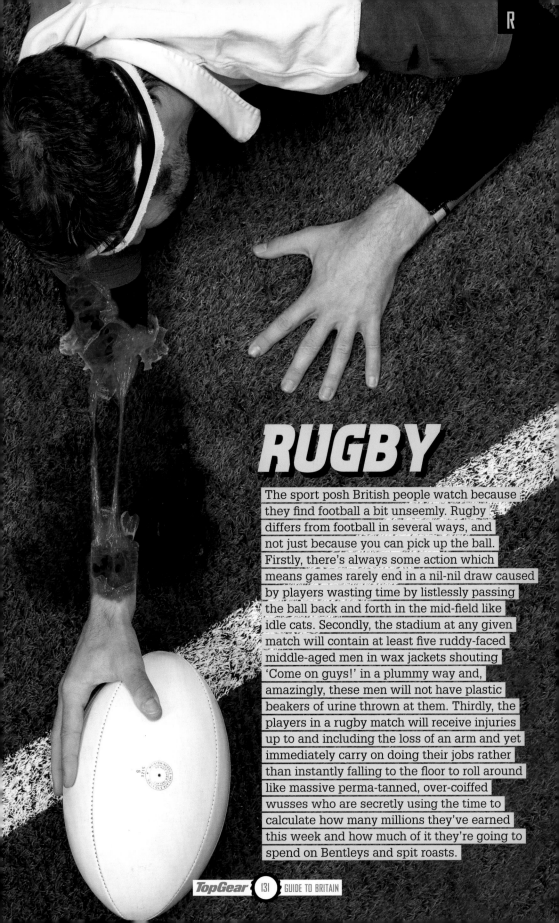

RUGBY

The sport posh British people watch because they find football a bit unseemly. Rugby differs from football in several ways, and not just because you can pick up the ball. Firstly, there's always some action which means games rarely end in a nil-nil draw caused by players wasting time by listlessly passing the ball back and forth in the mid-field like idle cats. Secondly, the stadium at any given match will contain at least five ruddy-faced middle-aged men in wax jackets shouting 'Come on guys!' in a plummy way and, amazingly, these men will not have plastic beakers of urine thrown at them. Thirdly, the players in a rugby match will receive injuries up to and including the loss of an arm and yet immediately carry on doing their jobs rather than instantly falling to the floor to roll around like massive perma-tanned, over-coiffed wusses who are secretly using the time to calculate how many millions they've earned this week and how much of it they're going to spend on Bentleys and spit roasts.

S SAYING GOODBYE

As a nation that thrives on tradition and protocol, the British are wedded to the correct process of saying goodbye. That's why farewells are peppered with phrases like 'take care', 'nice to see you' and 'see you soon' which are the small, polite steps that lead a British person towards the actual act of saying goodbye and leaving the room, hanging up the telephone or driving off. Without them, you would so brusque and rude that you might as well speak German.

SCOTLAND

A country at the northern extremity of Britain responsible for inventing many of the things we now take for granted in the modern world as well providing Great Britain with a disproportionate number of its politicians, comedians and football pundits. Scotland's rugged landscape and harsh climate makes the Scots a tough breed and a great many of them demonstrate this toughness by moving to London, not because they want to enter politics, comedy or football punditry, but because they want to be in the best position possible for whenever the Scottish decide to have another crack at their single most favoured pastime – kicking the shit out of the English.

SELF-CONFIDENCE

As a nation the British are extremely confident, but only with the benefit of at least 20 years of retrospect. Hence the British can be extremely bullish about when they had an empire or when they won the Second World War but ask them about their prospects for a forthcoming occasion such as an international sports fixture or the staging of a global event and their natural position will be to assume that, as a nation, they'll make a total cock of it. See: Olympics, The

YESTERYEAR'S EXPRESS

THE WORLD'S MOST SENTIMENTAL NEWSPAPER

13th April 2013 (but wouldn't it be great if it was 1956)

40p Can you remember when it was only 10p? Those were the days

FREE FOR EVERY READER!
ALL 3 MILLION EPISODES OF THE ARCHERS ON ONE DISC!

BRING BACK RATIONBOOKS

SENTIMENTALITY

Britain can be as effortlessly modern as sitting inside a minimalist glass cube designing an app. Unfortunately, Britain can also be a dreadfully mawkish place that gets needlessly sentimental about the past and clings to things from bygone times even though many of them were rubbish. To this day there is a faction in Britain that believe that the country's best days are behind it and thus every effort should be made to ensure that the entire place looks and acts like it's 1956. It's more commonly known as the *Daily Express*. See also; *Archers, The*

SHORT-SLEEVED SHIRTS

Cretinously unnecessary gentleman's upper garment much favoured by Audi-driving sales rep berks and rendered particularly moronic if paired with a tie. The short-sleeved shirt is the mark of an idiot since if the wearer weren't an idiot they would have realised they could have bought a normal shirt and simply rolled up the sleeves as required.

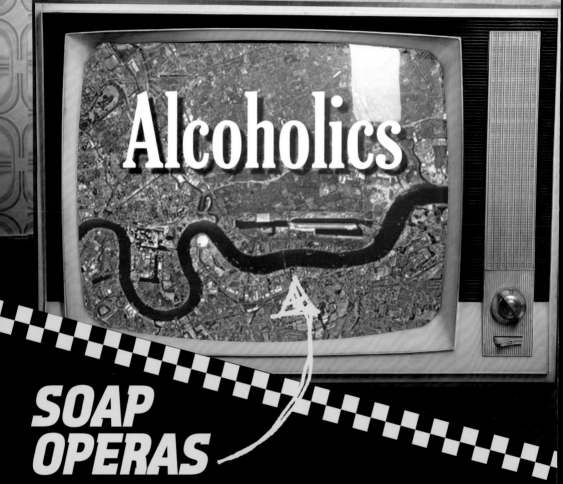

SOAP OPERAS

Ongoing television series extremely popular in Britain because the British love nothing more than watching the exploits of some fictional characters in one of the country's large urban areas, all of whom are extremely miserable and spend so much time in the pub that they must be functioning alcoholics.

SOLUTIONS

Idiotic and almost meaningless word, now hijacked by 70 percent of British businesses in the mistaken belief that it makes them sound more interesting when in fact it simply confirms that they are run by the kind of blithering simpletons who say 'yourself' when they mean 'you'.

http://www

Search

Business solutions   Search

Happy Woof Dog Walker
Canine activity and exercise **solutions**.

Bin Men
Providing your refuse disposal unit emptying **solutions**.

Green Lane Newsagent
Newspaper, greeting card, confectionery and fags **solutions**.

Dinner Ladies
Creating your educational establishment sustenance provision **solutions**.

Grimley's Abattoirs
Animal termination and dismantling **solutions**.

SPAGHETTI BOLOGNESE

A meal so ingrained in British culture that it has basically become British and its overseas inventors should probably just concede that it's not theirs any more, like a sort of meaty version of the Elgin Marbles. The great thing about spaghetti bolognese is that it can be made by pretty much anyone who can whack a load of mince and tomatoes into a pan and then boil up some spaghetti. That said, there are many variations on the basic theme and everyone in Britain believes their variation is unquestionably the best, even if it's got raspberries and cat food in it.

Traditional

BRITISH FOOD

Served all day!
12-3

Today's Special

SPAGHETTI BOLOGNESE!

PROVIDES NONE OF YOUR 5 A DAY!

DEFINITELY HAS SOME FORM OF MEAT IN IT!

DON'T GO ON HOLIDAY WITHOUT IT!

SPAM

American tinned meat that has become a totem of British life, partly because of a famous Monty Python sketch and partly because thin slices of highly processed meat taste best when placed between two limp pieces of white bread and eaten from a Tupperware container whilst sitting in a drizzle-flecked Ford Escort overlooking an especially grey segment of the North Sea. Or, as the British call it, 'on holiday'.

SPITFIRE

A fighter aircraft from the Second World War, the sight and sound of which is capable of making British people moist-eyed and lump-throated. Also the name of a frequently malfunctioning British sports car capable of eliciting the same reaction but for entirely different reasons.

SPORT

Sport is an important part of British life, assuming many forms and taking place in many different arenas. There are several things that drive the British devotion to sport in all its forms, ranging from the health benefits of some regular amateur activity to the inspirational and entertaining endeavours of professional sports people. However, the main driving force behind most British sports and the thing that brings that greatest national pleasure is very simple – seeing how annoyed Australia gets when we beat them again.

STEEPLES

Vital part of many British churches, without which they wouldn't look even half as churchy. Unfortunately, steeples seem to be in a stage of almost constant disrepair, necessitating some sort of appeal and the receipt of charitable donations in order to mend them. As a result, steeples are entirely responsible for the ongoing prosperity of the British enormous-mock -thermometer industry.

STIFF UPPER LIP

Keeping your emotions in check and steadfastly not making a fuss even in the face of vast personal tragedy, injury or suffering is seen as an entirely admirable thing in Britain. In fact, showing a stiff upper lip is an absolutely essential part of being British and what separates the people of Britain from their wildly gesticulating, openly weeping European neighbours. The only nation that can beat Britain for absolute emotional resolution at all times is Finland, a country where even tear-jerking events such as marriage proposals are kept as monosyllabically minimalist as possible. Other nations may find that repressed. The British regard it with utter admiration (although of course they don't show it).

SWIMMING

The British are very fond of swimming and many Britons like nothing more than visiting a municipal swimming pool where they may enjoy an hour of splashing about in the water and then two days of being convinced their skin still smells of chlorine. The only thing that can mar their enjoyment of this pastime is the belief that you shouldn't go swimming for an hour after eating, something that has largely been discredited but which was so drilled into every British person as a child that it's almost impossible for anyone in Britain to really relax and enjoy a swim until a good 90 minutes after lunch, just to be on the safe side.

T

TABLOID SPEAK

Within British English there are many linguistic sub-sets and one of the most familiar is Tabloid Speak. This bizarre language revolves inexplicable terms like 'love nest', 'steamy romp', 'busty beauty' and referring to any amount of money over £500 as 'cool'. Tabloid Speak only works when written down in a tabloid newspaper and cannot be used in normal conversation because it will make you sound like a boggle-eyed lunatic.

TEA, A NICE CUP OF

Warm, comforting, friendly, a nice cup of tea is basically British soul food. Indeed, there is almost no problem in Britain that can't be solved with a nice cup of tea, at or least made a little bit less severe. Tea enthusiast James May neatly sums up the British attitude to tea since, even if he was standing in the middle of the Gobi desert and the temperature was nudging 50 in the shade, he would be unable to resist the offer of a nice cup of tea. Unless he already had one on the go, and even then he'd have to think twice.

Minutes of War Cabinet emergency meeting,
26 May 1940

Churchill: Gentlemen, I have grave news from the continent. Our forces have been driven back towards the coast of France and, I regret to say, the Germans have us surrounded at Dunkirk. We must face the terrible prospect that within the next few hours it is likely that many tens of thousands of our men will be captured or killed.

Lord Halifax: This is dreadful news Prime Minister. Erm, would it help if someone were to put the kettle on?

Churchill: Yes. That would be nice.

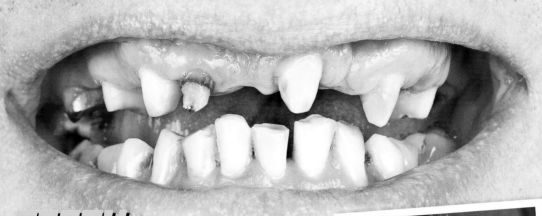

TEETH

Ask an American to think of something that is simultaneously revolting and amusing about the British and, without question, they will say 'teeth'. And yes, compared to the Americans, with their perfectly aligned and blindingly white smiles, the average British person's mouth does look like a beige scale model of an abandoned graveyard. Unless you're Richard Hammond.

THE THE

British band formed entirely to confuse people who alphabetise their music collections.

THINGS PEOPLE WHO WORK IN BRITISH HOTELS SAY

For some reason, the people who work in British hotels speak in an extremely odd way, sort of like a robot making a ham-fisted attempt at being polite. Hence, it is almost impossible to stay at a hotel in Britain without hearing linguistic carnage such as 'Will sir be breakfasting with us?', 'Would madam like to look at the lunch items?' and 'Has yourself taken advantage of our full leisure facilities?' No one knows where this bizarre way of speaking originated from but it's sodding idiotic and it needs to stop.

TRAINS

The British like trains. Indeed, in the past many British men liked trains so much they would stand at the end of station platforms and watch them go by before noting their serial numbers down in a book. This quaint habit has waned in the last few years, largely due to Operation Yewtree.

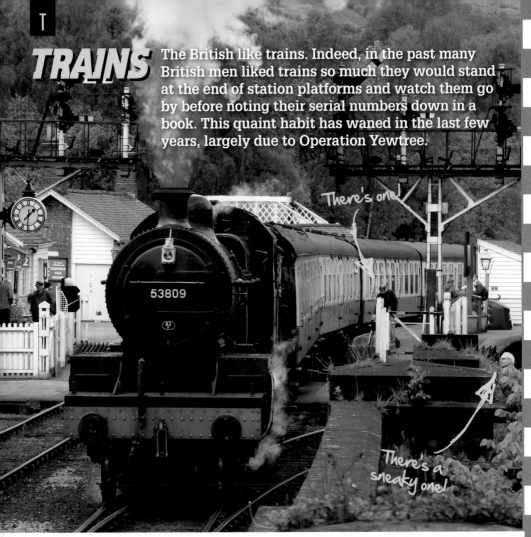

There's one!

There's a sneaky one!

TRAINS BASED ON CARS

Another ingenious idea from the white heat of the cauldron of the crucible of the anvil of the zenith of the apex of the genius of the *Top Gear* Technology Centre (rail division). Also, unusually, one that worked. Sort of.

TRENDY

A word used to mean 'fashionable' but only by people who aren't. Usually your dad.

TRIUMPH

Deceased British car maker, once known for its smart-looking and appealing range of models, not least the grunty and stylish TR6 sports car. Sadly, somewhere along the way Triumph made the tactical mistake of becoming part of British Leyland and was eventually powerless to resist becoming rubbish and then dead. The Triumph name, however, is still used by a maker of excellent British motorcycles, though they're nothing to do with the long-disappeared car company. Possibly for the best.

HUD 638L

TROUSERS

In the United States the garments that cover your legs are called 'pants', and this choice of word can also be heard not only in many other English-speaking nations, but also in those who have learned English as a second language. The British are actually rather pleased to know that other English speakers have not yet worked out that 'pants' isn't a funny word and 'trousers' emphatically is. Trousers. See? Trousers.

TUBE, THE

Nickname for London's underground rail network, as well as catch-all excuse-making shorthand for any lateness amongst people who live in the capital eg "Sorry I missed the Christening. Tch! The Tube!" Also explains why Londoners are so frequently sweaty and very cross.

twas

TVR

Blackpudlian maker of noisy, unruly and almost permanently malfunctioning sports cars for the terminally insane. Company later sold to a mysterious Russian business boy who managed to pilot the whole endeavour into the sea. A valuable lesson in car-company management. If you're trying to make a success of things, don't give the controls to someone who hasn't started shaving yet.

TWASP

The British very much enjoy swearing and part of the reason for this is because they have such a rich buffet of swearwords to choose from. Sadly, however, as attitudes and conventions evolve, many words that were once taboo have become less shocking, thereby diminishing their power when required to convey your feelings when you shut your hand in a door or need to describe the man who has just stolen your parking space. That is why the people of Britain need some new swearwords, starting with 'twasp'. Unfortunately, 'twasp' is so rude that we cannot tell you what it means because to do so would instantly have this book banned from sale. But trust us, it's pretty strong. So use twasp sparingly, with responsibility and not in polite company. Basically, just don't be a twasp about it.

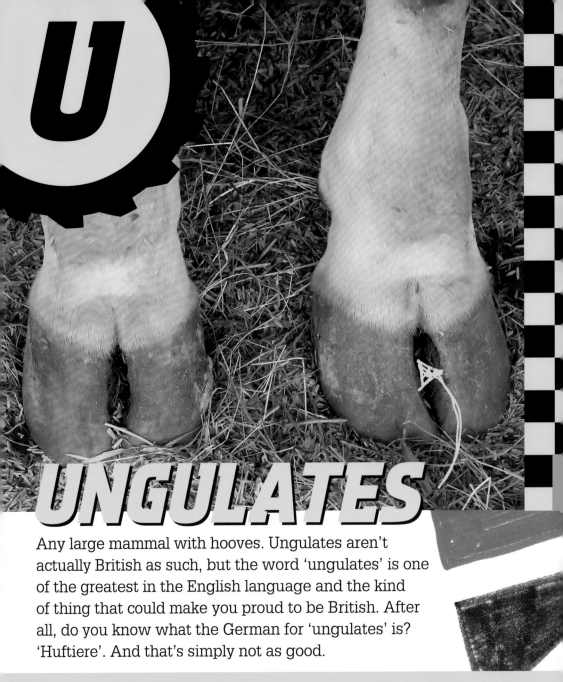

U

UNGULATES

Any large mammal with hooves. Ungulates aren't actually British as such, but the word 'ungulates' is one of the greatest in the English language and the kind of thing that could make you proud to be British. After all, do you know what the German for 'ungulates' is? 'Huftiere'. And that's simply not as good.

OTHER GREAT, LESSER SPOTTED BRITISH WORDS

Tmesis	Inserting a word into the middle of another word. For example, 'abso-bloody-lutely'.
Crepuscular	Of animals, to be most active around dawn and/or dusk.
Petrichor	The smell you get after it rains on a dry day.
Litotes	Using understatement for effect. The opposite of the verb 'to Clarkson'.
Twasp	Don't even ask

UNION JACK

The national flag of Great Britain, sometimes called the Union Flag by pedants who point out that 'Union Jack' only applies when the flag is being used by the Royal Navy. Such discussions are ignoring the more important fact that, whatever you call it, this is single greatest flag in the history of the world. While other countries labour under their unimaginative tricolours or their flags with idiotically complicated designs in the middle, the Union Jack effortlessly trumps all with its simple primary colours and striking, iconic design. Only the United States gets close, and could a child draw the Stars & Stripes with a just a red and a blue biro? Well, technically yes. But it would take them bloody ages. You could knock up a Union Flag in 10 seconds and it would still look ace. So there.

TOP FACT

Since the 2012 Olympics it's been okay to enjoy the Union Jack again without looking like a racist.

UNIONS

Organisations set up to defend the rights of workers, apart from in the 1970s when they were organisations dedicated to getting the workers to stand outside their place of work holding placards and lighting braziers rather than going inside to, say, loosely assemble some Austin Allegros.

MORE BRAZIERS NOW!

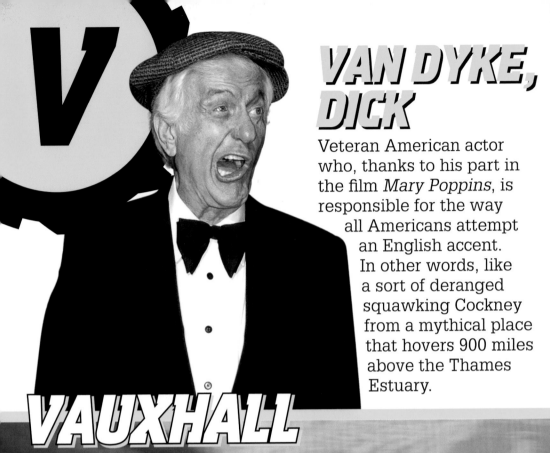

VAN DYKE, DICK

Veteran American actor who, thanks to his part in the film *Mary Poppins*, is responsible for the way all Americans attempt an English accent. In other words, like a sort of deranged squawking Cockney from a mythical place that hovers 900 miles above the Thames Estuary.

VAUXHALL

Once a proud maker of quality motoring cars and tasty treats like the Chevette HSR, Vauxhall gradually gave up its Luton-based independence and allowed itself to sell rebadged cars from Opel in Germany, leading inexorably to the grim cackfest of the ghastly mid-'90s Vectra. In the world of treasured national car-makers who aren't actually British, Vauxhall are forever playing second fiddle to Ford, not least because Ford's RS and ST models have long been the very definition of desirable, affordable hot hatches and saloons, whilst a fast Vauxhall sounds like something you would go out of your way to avoid.

JLA 250V

VESPA

Small Italian scooter much enjoyed by fashionable urbanites and not enjoyed at all by Jeremy Clarkson during *Top Gear*'s Vietnam special. In an unrelated calculation, James May once worked out that it would take a well-dispersed fleet of just a few hundred typically noisy Vespas ridden by a few hundred surly Italian teenagers to keep an entire nation awake well into the early hours of the morning.

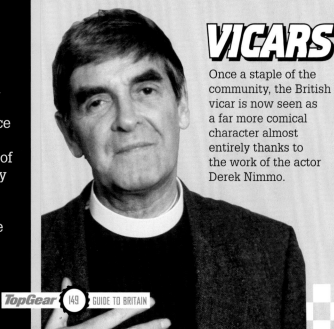

VICARS

Once a staple of the community, the British vicar is now seen as a far more comical character almost entirely thanks to the work of the actor Derek Nimmo.

VICTORIANS

What British people were called from the years 1837 to 1901. The Victorian era was a long and extremely influential period during which Britain was crammed with vastly bearded men, extremely starchy women and snub-nosed, consumption-wracked children. Victorian Britain was also known for its uptight manners, ill-matched bicycle wheels and proliferation of small tables, the sole purpose of which was to provide somewhere to put tiny brown photographs of extremely old women looking miserable. Mercifully, much of this Victoriana has disappeared leaving us just the pleasant and reassuringly sturdy houses.

VOLES

Small rodents, the protection and re-homing of which is responsible for delaying 64 percent of all British building projects. The other 36 percent are delayed by newts.

W

WAHEY!

Jaunty expression of surprise, delight or amusement popularised by TV presenter Keith 'Cheggers' Chegwin. Ergo, the catchphrase of a former alcoholic and best avoided.

WALES

Hilly country on the left-hand side of Britain and home to TV's Richard Hammond (almost). Unlike England and Scotland, Wales has never exported its social culture overseas which is why you will never see a Welsh theme pub in foreign climes. And even if you did it would only have close harmony choir singing on the jukebox and you wouldn't want to stay for long. One reason given for this insularity is that, at a time when the Scottish and English (and indeed the Irish) were abandoning their home lands and emigrating, the Welsh had realised they were sitting on valuable reserves of coal and gold which persuaded them to stay at home. The real reason, however, is that because it always rains in Wales and their phlegmy language causes everyone to be drenched in spit during conversation, the Welsh are kept permanently moist and cannot go to warmer countries for fear of drying out.

WALKING HOLIDAYS

Classically British break, very popular in bygone times because it included three things the British used to enjoy very much; camping, drizzle and not going abroad. Thankfully, those times are past. Unless you are Richard Hammond, in which case you can think of literally nothing better than a week yomping through mud and sleeping in a canvas sack somewhere in an especially wet bit of the Lake District.

WAN'AAAAAAAAR

A quaint Cockney word often used by van drivers. It roughly translates as 'Your manner of driving has displeased me, sir'.

WAR

War is a brutal, terrible, often senseless thing. Yet it would be impossible to deny that the British rather like it. In particular, the British are very fond of reminiscing about wars of the past, especially the ones they won, which was most of them. This last thing may go some way to explaining why Britain secretly loves a good war. It's the same as drinking, swearing and beating the Australians at sport. The British like it because they're good at it. *See also; fighting*

GALES

Chucking It Down

-5

GALES

Blizzards!

15

Nice Out

Well Sweaty!

GALES

Bit Parky

-10

Brass Monkeys

1

10

32

Windy

24

Brrrrrr

WEATHER, THE

People from abroad believe that the British are obsessed with the weather and they are of course correct. In fact, over 37 percent of all conversations in Britain are about the weather. This may seem strange to someone from, say, Rome or Los Angeles but that's because the weather in Rome or Los Angeles is broadly predictable. And to people from warm and predictable climes, talking endlessly about the weather seems as strange as starting every interaction by talking at length and with enthusiasm about the colour of a glass of water. But that's to forget that the weather in Britain is wildly variable and the equivalent of turning on the tap to fill your glass uncertain if what came out would be scorching hot, icy cold or unexpectedly grey. You'd talk about that, now wouldn't you? Exactly.

How to talk about the weather in a British way

Guests at, say, a classic British bed & breakfast know that upon arriving in the dining room for breakfast, the conversation with other British people must proceed as follows:

- Good morning

- General remark about the weather

- Jaunty follow-up remark about the weather and/or surroundings (optional)

- Conversation may now end

WEST COUNTRY, THE

Lower western extreme of England known for agriculture, cider consumption and belief amongst rest of Britain that they use 'wife' as a synonym for 'sister'.

WITCHELL, NICHOLAS

Currently the BBC's royal correspondent, a position he holds even though Prince Charles, the actual heir to the throne, has been captured on tape expressing utter disdain for him. Ergo, a classically British example of social and professional awkwardness on a grandly institutional level.

WOMEN'S INSTITUTE, MILITIA WING OF THE

They try to claim there isn't one, but there is. They make fruit cake with explosives in it and sell oven gloves with extremely provocative statements on them.

X

X5

Large BMW-made vehicle in what Americans would call the 'sports utility' style. A triumph of German engineering and one of the first tall, 4x4 machines to boast the performance and handling of a car. Unfortunately, all of this is irrelevant in Britain where every X5 sports a ghastly private number plate that needlessly repeats its model name and is almost certainly driven by a total bellend.

XYLOPHONE

Plinky wooden musical instrument and what all A-Zs put in this section because there's not much else that starts with X. Unless you're in Croatia, where the word for 'xylophone' is 'ksilofon'. In which case, your A-Z is knackered.

YES (MEANING NO)

The British love of politeness means that many times when someone says 'yes' they really mean 'Oh dear God, no' but can't say so for fear of offending. Have a look at the faces of everyone on an outward-bound course or at a pyramid-selling seminar or giving their bank details to those charity people in bright tabards who ambush you in the street. Those are the faces of people who have politely said yes when they meant no.

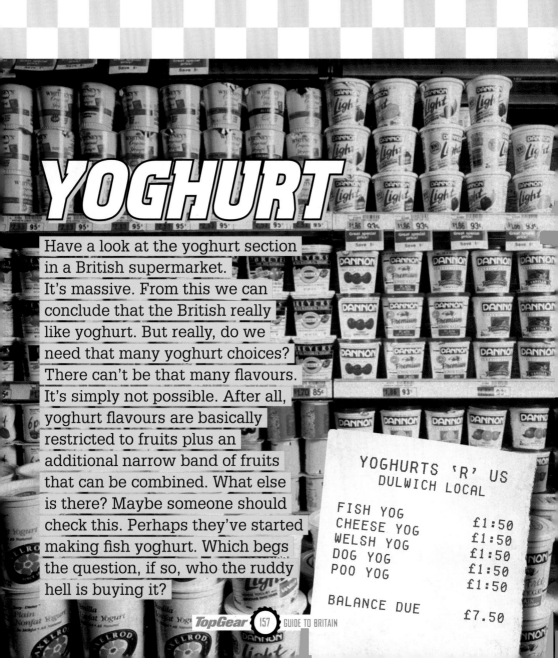

YOGHURT

Have a look at the yoghurt section in a British supermarket. It's massive. From this we can conclude that the British really like yoghurt. But really, do we need that many yoghurt choices? There can't be that many flavours. It's simply not possible. After all, yoghurt flavours are basically restricted to fruits plus an additional narrow band of fruits that can be combined. What else is there? Maybe someone should check this. Perhaps they've started making fish yoghurt. Which begs the question, if so, who the ruddy hell is buying it?

YOGHURTS 'R' US DULWICH LOCAL	
FISH YOG	£1:50
CHEESE YOG	£1:50
WELSH YOG	£1:50
DOG YOG	£1:50
POO YOG	£1:50
BALANCE DUE	£7.50

YORKSHIRE

English county that gave us Jeremy Clarkson (born in Doncaster), Richard Hammond (brought up in Ripon) and James May (brought up in Rotherham). Strangely, none of them lives there now.

YORKSHIRE CARS
Volkswagen Golf GTaye
Citroen T'CV
BMW By 'ecks5
Mercedes Eeeeeee-class
Jeep Grand Cherokee

Z

ZEPHANIAH, BENJAMIN

Birmingham-born, devotedly left-wing street poet, vegetarian and animal rights campaigner. Never been a guest on *Top Gear*, strangely.

ZEAL, MONACHORUM

Devon village and the single greatest place name in Britain. Mostly because it sounds like a Bond villain or a strange disease that makes cows' knees go funny.

ZESTY

The kind of word that is used, and can only be used, during a wine tasting. As long as you accept that it makes you sound like a bit of a twasp.

1 3 5 7 9 10 8 6 4 2

First published in 2013 by BBC Books, an imprint of Ebury Publishing
A Random House Group Company

Text © Richard Porter 2013

Top Gear (word marks and logos) is a trademark of the British Broadcasting Corporation and used under licence. Top Gear © 2005

All rights reserved. No part of this publication may be reproduced, stored in a retrieval system, or transmitted in any form or by any means, electronic, mechanical, photocopying, recording or otherwise, without the prior permission of the copyright owner.

The Random House Group Limited Reg. No. 954009

Addresses for companies within the Random House Group can be found at www.randomhouse.co.uk

A CIP catalogue record for this book is available from the British Library.

ISBN: 978 1 849 90690 6

The Random House Group Limited supports the Forest Stewardship Council® (FSC®), the leading international forest-certification organisation. Our books carrying the FSC label are printed on FSC®-certified paper. FSC is the only forest-certification scheme supported by the leading environmental organisations, including Greenpeace. Our paper procurement policy can be found at www.randomhouse.co.uk/environment

Commissioning editor: Lorna Russell
Project editor: Joe Cottington
Picture researchers: Claire Gouldstone and Giles Chapman
Design: Amazing15
Production: Antony Heller

Colour origination by Amazing15
Printed and bound in Germany by Firmengruppe APPL, aprinta druck, Wemding, Germany

To buy books by your favourite authors and register for offers visit www.randomhouse.co.uk

Picture credits

BBC Books would like to thank the following individuals and organizations for providing photographs and for permission to reproduce copyright material. While every effort has been made to trace and acknowledge copyright holders, we would like to apologize should there be any errors or omissions.

BBC Worldwide Ltd: 5, 9 (t), 9 (b), 14 (t), 15 (t), 16, 17, 22 (inset), 34, 35 (l), 37 (b, inset), 38 (cl, cr, b), 42 (b), 45 (t), 54, 64, 66, 71 (inset), 72-73, 76 (bl), 78-79, 81 (bl), 83 (t), 94 (br), 96 (b), 108 (t), 116 (t), 126 (cr), 130 (b), 137 (b), 140, 142 (b), 149 (t), 150 (c, inset), 152 (inset); **Giles Chapman Library**: p21 (bl, br), p54, p62 (b), p85 (b), p88, p93 (t), p96 (c), 99, 101 (t), 106-107 (b), 121 (tr), 126 (t and c), 128 (b), 129 (b), 143 (c), 148 (b), 156 (t); **Corbis**/Gideon Mendel 113 (t); **Alamy**: /Matthew Richardson 7 (b), /Motoring Picture Library 124, /Squint 121, /Matt Cardy 36 (t), Kathy deWitt 159 (t); **Getty**: 102 (b), /James Keyser/Time Life Images 157, /Michael Ochs Archives 90 (t), SambaPhoto/Izan Petterie 86, Popperfoto 82 (b), /Tim Whitby 90 (l), /Oli Scarff (b), /David Montgomery 25 (t), /WireImage 148 (t), /Kevin Cummins 151, /Frederick M. Brown/Stringer 86 (inset), /Tom O'Donnell 90 (c), /Pier Marco Tacca 27, /Antony Jones (b), 74 (l), /David Levenson 119, /meshaphoto 114, /Mark Cuthbert 74 (cr), 155 (c); **Rex**: /Brian Rasic 74 (r), /Jonathan Player 74 (cl), /David Hartley 38 (t), /ITV 149 (b), /Ken Towner/ Evening Standard 16, /Dan Wooller 58 (t), /Universal/Everett 58 (c). All other images **Shutterstock**.